The Leadership VACCINE

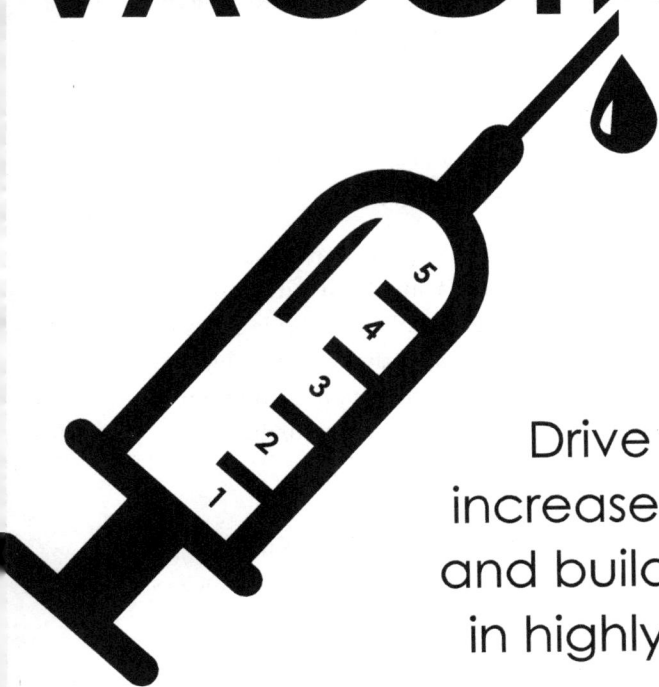

Drive **innovation**, increase **efficiency** and build **resilience** in highly regulated industries

REBECCA GODFREY PhD

RƎTHINK PRESS

First published in Great Britain in 2020
by Rethink Press (www.rethinkpress.com)

© Copyright Rebecca Godfrey

Contents

Introduction   **1**

The five pillars of The Leadership Vaccine   5

Why this is important   9

Meet Tom   13

1   **Heavy Is The Head That Wears The Crown**   **15**

TBB – the little company that could   18

Two weeks earlier: TBB's Team Strategy day   20

The present day   23

The clique   27

Keeping the momentum going   29

Tom's change of heart   33

Summary   35

2   **Leadership Blind Spots**   **39**

Staff interactions   43

A revealing tour of the office   49

Summary   51

3 Value   **53**

Abdication over delegation   56

Personality preferences   59

How we interact with the world around us   63

Every business needs all preferences   64

A few weeks later   68

Summary   70

4 Advocate Part One   **73**

Belonging versus fitting in   74

Vision, mission and values   77

Creating a mission statement   84

How to motivate   86

Summary   90

5 Advocate Part Two   **93**

Groupthink   94

Dinner in Abilene   98

Group development   105

Summary   112

6 Clarify   **115**

The power of niching   116

Transparency wins   120

How to start clarifying scope   123

Scope paralysis   128

A week later   133

Reflections   135

Summary   139

7 Create   **143**

It's a familiar story   144

My next meeting with Tom   146

The RACI matrix   150

Building in resilience   154

Summary   160

8 Inspire   **163**

Sarah's story   166

One-to-ones   168

Co-Co plots   172

A little respect   177

We all need a battle plan   181

Summary   185

9 Enable   **189**

Gain oversight through a process inventory 191

KPIs   199

Root cause analysis   200

Developing CAPA plans   203

Summary   206

10 Execute   **209**

The one-year anniversary   211

Culture   212

Scope   216

Structure   217

Staff development   218

Process   219

Summary   223

Conclusion   **226**

Appendix   **229**

References   **231**

Acknowledgements   **233**

The Author   **237**

*For Mark, Ethan and Theo, my beautiful,
inspiring and hilarious little family.*

Introduction

Developing leaders is essential, not only for the benefit of the teams they lead and the businesses to whom their talent is invaluable, but also for the leaders themselves. Often many of the qualities for which we were hired in the early stages of our career – detail oriented, focused, precise – are somewhat contrary to those we need in leadership – visionary, flexible, adaptable. Consequently, leadership development is a vital area that requires specific investment, not only financially, but also in terms of time – time to learn and develop key skills and behaviours in order to lead, build, grow and inspire teams.

In highly regulated industries, we are driven by the desire to innovate and progress scientifically and/or technologically to bring much needed, often life-changing solutions to the customers we serve. At the same time, we need to maintain strict compliance with complex and ever-evolving regulations. As a result, our organisations and teams are commonly shaped organically. Altogether this leads to particular challenges for leaders. These include:

The constant need to fire-fight: The need to be flexible, agile and in a position to respond to changes in regulation, organisation, or as a result of the outcome of experimentation, data analysis and so on. Such changes are often so frequent that we are still dealing with or implementing the last change when the next arrives, so we don't have the time or space to proactively consider, plan or resource for upcoming changes until they are upon us.

Not only are we under pressure personally, but we are leading a team experiencing similar challenges, each team member looking to us to chart the course and steer the ship.

Balancing conflicting priorities: Due to the complex, global and interlaced nature of our business, roles and responsibilities within a process, product or project often span teams, departments, offices and, in some cases, organisations. As if dealing with the conflicting priorities of innovation and compliance weren't enough, each team has multiple stakeholders with their own priorities, timelines and needs. As an individual, balancing these priorities can be tough; as a leader, it can feel impossible sometimes.

Stretched resources in the team: For many of us as leaders, the greatest challenge, more often than not, is that we don't have enough time, enough budget and/or enough human resources. These challenges increase in an environment where there is rarely a status quo – constant change and innovation brings with it an additional resource strain for us.

When we first become a leader, we often feel that we're expected to have all of the answers and be unshakable. We put ourselves under huge pressure, believing we're under the constant gaze of high expectations by which competencies are measured. Over the years, as we continue to take on more and more responsibility, we tend to become increasingly confident and realise that our role as a leader isn't actually to know everything. Rather, it is more about being available to our team, having the confidence to say, 'I don't know everything, but let's work this out together', and knowing enough to ask the right questions.

Some of the most competent leaders I've met are the ones with the confidence to say, 'I have no clue', but their teams always know that they will work together to find out. My most rewarding leadership roles have been when I've worked with my team, who knew exactly what they could expect from me. They knew they could count on me, and I knew what I could count on them to do. This was the realisation that leadership was not something I had to do alone. I was the leader, but I was a leader of people, and those people were on my side. It was my duty to bring them with me, to raise them up so we would deliver great work together.

Sadly, we tend to look at leadership development as a course, workshop or classroom-based activity where we learn principles, receive advice or the latest in leadership theory over one, two or five days, and then head back to work to get on with our role. But when did anyone ever learn effectively this way?

Surely, we learn not by simply being told, but by trying and failing; by stumbling and overcoming. We need to allow our leaders space to fail, while all the time providing the structure and support so that this failure isn't fatal to their confidence or resulting in lasting damage to business. But how do we build resilience in our leadership without jeopardising the business?

Firstly, we need to get better at educating our leaders, not just training them. We need to share principles, insights and tools, and then encourage further development through time spent away from the classroom to work through on-the-job activities; to try, fail and ultimately succeed, thereby allowing individuals the chance to develop their own leadership style and, importantly, their confidence.

It's fallacy to believe that leaders are born and not made. When we hear of 'born leaders', often they are particularly strong at garnering excitement, building the team culture and providing fantastic staff-development opportunities. Scratch below the surface, though, and you may find that although the team members are excited and passionate about what they are doing, they aren't really clear on the boundaries of their responsibilities. Are they owning their processes? How resilient is the team if strong leadership is not available?

The five pillars of The Leadership Vaccine

During my leadership journey, I was fortunate enough to experience many wonderful successes. My teams and I made significant positive changes to our organisation, in some cases on a global scale, all the time forging strong working relationships with our stakeholders. I'd like to say that these successes were hard to achieve. There is no doubt that they required hard work, focus and determination, but I would never describe them as 'hard', because when things worked, they just seemed smooth, easy and natural.

As I write this, I imagine I sound like I have had a smooth journey with no blips – oh, but there were blips and failures aplenty. When I started to reflect on my successes and failures, I was curious to better understand what allowed my team and I to achieve what had previously seemed impossible. How did we make such positive change so smoothly? Why did the failures happen and what were we doing differently that resulted in either success or failure? The failures certainly weren't due to a lack of effort, want, or blood, sweat and tears!

This curiosity led me to map out the various activities, processes, initiatives, procedures and practices we'd implemented in each of the leadership roles that I had held where we had achieved significant success, or had seen failure, from small niche consultancy to Top-10 pharma. I cannot express the surprise I felt when I realised that all along, there had simply been five things – or 'pillars', as I now refer to them – that made the difference.

These five pillars are:

1. Culture – building the right culture within the team that's aligned to that of the organisation. Setting direction and fostering trust through the development of a team purpose, vision for the future and shared team values. Allowing the team members to know what they stand for and where they are going.

2. Scope – developing and maintaining a clear view on the scope and boundaries of the team's responsibilities and activities. Ensuring seamless links between interfacing organisations and teams, thereby removing gaps and/or duplication in cross-functional projects and processes. Allowing the team members to know clearly what they do and where their responsibilities start and stop.

3. Structure – creating the right organisational struc-ture, not only in terms of the organisation chart itself, but also in mindset. Removing hierarchical constraints and ensuring empowerment of all team members. Establishing subject-matter expertise and accountability at all levels within the team. Allowing for distributed control in an environment where each party knows their role within the team.

4. Staff development – implementing appropriate staff-development methodologies which not only support individuals' skills and knowledge, but also their confidence. Empowering team members to continuously improve themselves, their processes and their outputs.

5. Processes – supporting and enabling the team to develop **robust, efficient and future-proofed end-to-end processes** with enhanced oversight, where issues and risks are identified early, mitigated pro-actively and lead to robust improvements. Allowing team members to have ownership of their processes, and the leader to have better oversight as a result.

It's rare that a leader is a 'natural' across all five of these different pillars, but to lead a truly resilient, high-performing team, we need time and space to develop across all five pillars to become a holistic and resilient leader.

The five pillars are central to The Leadership Vaccine methodology that I share with you in this book. Just as a vaccine arms the body with immunity and resilience against disease, The Leadership Vaccine arms leaders with clarity, certainty and confidence in their role, allowing them to develop empowered, engaged and inspired teams who are enabled to flex and innovate in the face of change.

In keeping with this metaphor, remember that we cannot vaccinate ourselves against everything through a jab alone; our environment also grants us the opportunity to develop immunity through picking up bugs along the way. Similarly, courses, training manuals and books cannot teach us everything we need to become a great leader. We must look at leadership development as an ever-evolving journey; there is no single definitive leadership profile. Our potential comes in many different guises.

Throughout the book, I will be unpacking each of the five pillars using a typical company as an example. The pillars are only truly effective when they operate as a whole, not as single doses, as each contains a value that impacts on the other four. As you follow our leader Tom and his team working their way through the five pillars, it will help you to gain fresh perspectives and clarity on both progress and direction, and at the end of each chapter, I'll summarise the ways in which Tom and his team have moved through the methodology. Ultimately, by working though The Leadership Vaccine, like Tom, you will develop the potential to ensure your teams will be more enabled, empowered and motivated than ever before to excel at their jobs. As a result, Tom and his team now love what they do, and I'm sure the same will happen for you and the people you lead.

Why this is important

I have worked in the wonderfully exciting, demanding and rewarding pharmaceutical industry since 2007, and it has been an incredible and unexpectedly personal journey. After a desperately short stint as a postdoctoral researcher, I joined the industry as a keen post-PhD scientist, knowing that the end goal of serving patients was important. But because I had never known anybody close to me to be diagnosed with a serious illness, that end goal always seemed somewhat abstract and more of a commercial imperative. The patient at that time was relatively faceless.

That all changed in October of 2014 when I received an unforgettable text from my dad:

> *'Beck, I've just been to the specialist to speak about my trapped nerve and they've told me that they think I have Motor Neurone Disease. Do you know what that is?'*

Sadly, I did know. I knew it was a terminal illness for which there was no cure, and little or no treatment. It's a cruel, evil and relentless disease, arriving with little warning and making its mark quickly and firmly.

When Dad was diagnosed, he only had a limp, so the last thing we were expecting from his doctor's appointment was for him to receive a death sentence – one that would come to pass after two-and-a-half years. Following Dad's diagnosis, I became clearer than ever before on the value my job, and my industry, had on its end customer. I also realised why life-work balance was absolutely essential. In spite of dealing with a high-risk pregnancy and wanting to be with my dad as much as possible, I still needed to turn up for work and serve my team, and ultimately the patients for whom our medicines were vital.

When not at work, I would spend endless hours online researching treatments, trials and tools that could spare Dad some of the pain and discomfort he was suffering. I would arrive at Dad's house with microwaveable slippers, jogging pants for wheelchair users and small, weird-shaped cushions to spare his sore knees, which knocked together as his leg muscles disappeared. I made a weekly pot of chicken pearl barley risotto as I knew it was one of the few meals he could still eat. I attended every consultant appointment, asking endless lists of questions to make sure Dad had what he needed.

As his disease progressed, I was lucky to be supported by my company by being allowed to work four longer days and spend a full day a week with Dad, taking him in his electric wheelchair, along with my son Ethan, three years old at the time, to Whipsnade Safari Park to watch the sea lion show. I was extremely fortunate in that I had a team which was cohesive, high performing and kind to one another. Within the team there was respect, engagement, motivation and support. Whenever someone had a tough time, be that professionally or personally, the rest of us had their back. Everybody was clear on what everyone else on the team was doing, so whenever I needed to take leave, I knew my team was confident enough to continue without me. For so long, my leadership career had been focused on supporting my team members, but when I needed them most, they supported me, and to them I am forever grateful.

A collective sense of empowerment enabled my team to build – with guidance, but without the need for my direct input – the most incredible processes that were respected by our colleagues around the world. I felt a real sense of achievement that I was doing a good job of empowering, developing, challenging and supporting my team, but at the same time, I could leave the office at the end of the day to deal with my own personal difficulties without bringing the work home with me. If that was good practice for me, that was also good practice for my team.

None of us can truly know what our colleagues are going through at home. Despite the fact they may choose, or not, to share their private lives, we must always be respectful of the fact that they *are* private, and that sometimes, life at home may be more difficult than any of us can imagine. It's unreasonable for leaders to expect people to come to work and fight battles when that doesn't need to be the case.

This kind of supportive working environment will depend on how we behave, respond and plan as leaders. Our job is surely more about inspiring the people around us than charging into battle every day. It's for this reason that I am so passionate about creating frameworks for leaders which build strong and positive cultures as foundations for people, and businesses, to survive and thrive. I take great pride and pleasure in seeing a notification pop up on LinkedIn that one of my former colleagues has been given a brilliant promotion, because my dream is that every person I've ever led will end up being more senior than I was when I led them. I'm delighted to say that dream is now coming to fruition. Nothing beats the feeling of knowing that I played a small part in their journey towards success and they will now get to experience leadership for themselves.

Perhaps that's one reason why you've picked up my book – to find out what you can learn about leadership from the inside track. I don't want this to be an academic book because leadership isn't academic, although I'd certainly encourage you to read some of the books or papers I list in the 'References' section at the end. This book is intended to appeal to your curiosity in emotional, while still practical, ways. I'm hoping it will give you 'aha' moments, because I've lived and experienced the highs and lows of leadership, and because leadership is about real life.

Meet Tom

To highlight The Leadership Vaccine in action, I've chosen a specific vehicle in this book which nicely illustrates the journey of somebody going through the methodology, learning from it and implementing it as they progress. I'm going to tell you the story of Tom Bryan, the founder and CEO of medical engineering consultancy, TBB Limited.[1]

There are aspects of Tom in all of us, so it's fascinating to see him progress through the methodology over a twelve-month period and the impact of him making changes – some of them small, but still powerful – as a result. His story offers valuable insights as we see him build connections with his team. When we first meet him, such connections are practically non-existent, not because he is a bad person – in fact, quite the opposite; Tom is one of the nicest and most approachable CEOs we might have the pleasure to encounter. However, because his team didn't know how nice he is, Tom, as

---

1   I should point out that Tom is not a real person as an individual; he is, in fact, a fictitious composite. The challenges and solutions that I've described in his story are illustrations of the experiences leaders across our industry are facing daily – those in big companies, small companies, customer-facing companies, in-house teams.

he later admits, having always been focused on the product or project, didn't know how to lead.

If you happen to be a leader of a group in a large business yourself, don't be tempted to think that the size of Tom's company has no relevance to your own, especially when I later talk about profit margins. In a big business, these correlate to efficiency, cost and time. The same challenges apply, no matter the size of your business, because when you consider compliance and timelines, every inefficiency adds up, each one having a compounding effect.

In a big pharma company, for example, if every team contributes towards even the smallest inefficiency, the impact overall on a clinical development programme, and ultimately the cost of medicines to the end user, is massive. That can mean the difference between medicines being available to patients or not. If each team were able to cut their cost by 2% over a company of 100,000 people, just imagine what the impact would be on the final cost of medicines.

It's the responsibility of every leader to look at the cost effectiveness of each of our teams. It's also the responsibility of every leader to be confident in our roles. Without this our people, our businesses and ultimately our customers will suffer.

ONE

Heavy Is The Head That Wears The Crown

25 July

I t was one of those rare, blisteringly hot July days which saw the temperature gauge in my car already registering 29°c at 10.45am as I left the M11 at Cambridge. No more than a few minutes later, I was walking across a sweltering car park towards a relatively new black glass-fronted incubator office development. Reflecting the glare of the sun, it dominated the science park where I was meeting at 11am with my recently acquired client, Tom Bryan, founder of TBB.

Entering through the sliding doors, I welcomed the relief from the scorching summer heat as I slipped into the air-conditioned communal reception area, where I signed in and waited to be met, a couple of minutes later, by Tom's PA, Ruth.

Taking the lift, we went past the fourth floor, entirely populated by TBB's operation, to the fifth, which housed a busy hive of meeting rooms and hubs shared by the block's residents: a mix of tech and scientific research enterprises. We made small talk about the weather and almost certainly about our respective holiday plans before Ruth announced that Tom was running a little behind schedule.

'He's in another meeting, but what's new?' she said with a chuckle of familiarity, followed by a quizzical glance to ensure I wasn't annoyed. I wasn't; I was already familiar with his erratic timekeeping patterns after only a handful of meetings. She assured me he wouldn't keep me waiting long as she ushered me into a large, light and airy conference room that was typically kitted out and offered me a drink, before leaving me alone with my thoughts.

I didn't mind; the delay gave me a chance to check my emails, although I have to say I was aware that our one hour together would be just that, without any possibility of going beyond our allotted time – and today, there was a lot to discuss. Tom's time, as I now knew, was a precious commodity, and in scarce supply. In his defence, I knew only too well from past experience how that felt: pulled from pillar to post, ready with late-running apologies that would trip off the tongue like they were second nature.

I'd only met Tom for the first time in person a few weeks prior to this. He'd originally contacted me, the result of a recommendation from a mutual client, as he was interested in me running one of my Team Strategy workshops for him and ten of his team members. The nature of these workshops allows everybody to talk for an equal amount of time, so whether they're introvert, extrovert, experienced, or not so confident, each has the opportunity to explore their ideas and put them on the table.

In the run up to the workshop, we'd had a few short meetings, but often I'd sensed I didn't have Tom's full attention. During our planning meetings, he'd interrupt to respond to a text message, an email, sign some paperwork, or deal with some other urgently pressing matter. He might have been present physically, but mentally he wasn't always in the room. It felt as if our work together was last-minute seat-of-your-pants planning, a tick-box exercise.

Planning was something Tom vaguely knew he needed to improve, while not being entirely clear as to why, but to his credit, he stuck with it. We eventually agreed to a full day's workshop, offsite, in which he wanted to run through the next three years' plans for the business with his team.

It was at that workshop that everything changed for Tom.

TBB – the little company that could

TBB had been running for five years by now, set up after Tom was made redundant from his position as director of projects in a mid-sized medical-device company. When his former employer found itself subject to a hostile takeover by a wealthier overseas corporation, Tom was suddenly surplus to requirements. His generous severance package and excellent relationships with former contacts presented him with a no-brainer opportunity to set up a small niche consultancy of his own.

Tom invested a significant portion of his funds into the enterprise, rented some serviced office space and employed a couple of trusted ex-colleagues. It was win-win as far as he was concerned: here he was, master of his own destiny, in complete control of both his strategic planning and processes. Furthermore, he was charging out his services at lucrative freelance rates well beyond his previous salary.

Within twelve months, Tom was reaping the rewards as the business and its reputation for excellence grew incrementally year on year. Also growing were his ambitions to scale, but five years down the line, that dream had run into a roadblock. Now, with fifty-five employees to look after and an impressive roster of clients to service, Tom was staring at the reality of being unable to raise the necessary investment to take the business to the next level, and things had started to slip.

Increasingly, the business was falling behind on vital contractual obligations for clients, which was proving to be problematic. Its reputation for consistent deliverability was regularly being called into question, even by its most loyal of service users, when at one time, it was considered to be the paragon of reliability and gold-medal standard. This doubt in his clients' eyes wasn't part of Tom's plan; his dream was to go to the next level, because the business was rapidly outgrowing being a niche consultancy.

When Tom and I met for the first time, TBB was sitting somewhat uncomfortably between other niche competitors and the guys with the bigger market share and bigger bucks. Either Tom could choose to do nothing at all and remain at the same level, or – worse – the business could retract. That was not an option.

'I want to go big, I want to get investment,' he was to tell me at our meeting today. 'But right now, with the daily chaos going on here and the way we currently operate, I know I don't have the right structures in place to make that happen. I hate to admit this, but it's true.'

It was clear that if he didn't do something to counter this, not only would the company stagnate, but the issues would escalate, and he'd have no choice but to move backwards. He was finally admitting he was struggling as a leader.

Two weeks earlier: TBB's Team Strategy day

The day itself began awkwardly. As the team members arrived and headed to the tea and coffee station, I could immediately feel a sense of resistance from them. Mutterings about 'A bloody waste of time', 'Better things to do', 'What's he playing at?' and 'Where's this all coming from?' reached my ears.

In their defence, I understood where all of these thoughts stemmed from. From my initial experience of working with Tom, I could imagine that the team was most likely operating pretty much in the dark when it came to planning for the future, unless they received a directive from Tom. As far as he was concerned, he'd invited me to run this workshop so that he could share with his team how they could tackle their new targets and the challenging performance-related three-year plans. His low engagement with me and huge ability to be distracted with all things business during the planning process hadn't fully prepared him, or his team, for what was about to emerge.

From a total workforce of fifty-five, Tom had selected ten to attend the day, ranging from members of his management team to team leaders, representing almost 20% of the workforce. Two of the management team, Rachel and David, both in their late thirties with results-driven personalities, resented the fact they'd been pulled away from their daily tasks to an offsite activity. They made it known that, as the top performers, they felt there was 'nothing to be gained' by dragging themselves away from their stations to sit around and talk nonsense when they could be back at base, making the business money.

At first, they were bending Tom's ear, but only moments later, all three of them were sharing a joke. Tom obviously liked them and thought of them as a team, although to the others, they looked more like the clique they actually were. As the day started, this trio and Chris, a big-picture-thinking extrovert who pitched in with some exciting and dynamic insights of his own, dominated the conversations, while the remainder of the attendees withdrew more into themselves as their voices were more or less ignored.

By mid-morning, we were diving deeper into the workshop and everybody was allocated an equal opportunity to voice their own thoughts and insights. I observed the familiar magic of the workshop beginning to work. Individuals, such as Sophie, the team leader from finance and admin, Jake, the head of quality, and Virginia, one of the documentation managers, began offering suggestions, challenging ideas and sharing thoughts that neither Tom nor his circle of trusted favourites had even considered before – ideas that could potentially remove, or prevent backlogs, in the chain of command.

Hearing them speak, I recognised their excitement and relief at being given the chance to not only contribute, but also be heard. These lightbulb moments took everyone by surprise, and because the ideas were inherently sensible, practicable and implementable, they ignited the whole group in an animated discussion that quite naturally brought it together as one unit. From starting the day as a disparate and disgruntled group, they showed potential for future cohesion as suddenly the vibe had shifted.

For the first time, Tom was actively taking notice of team members' opinions, acutely aware that it wasn't just those closest to him who could generate effective and productive ideas. As the workshop drew to a close, everyone present sensed a positive change in the atmosphere and group dynamic. Then I asked everyone how they felt the day had gone. There was a palpable excitement in the air as they responded, talking about what they'd discussed, learned and offered to each other.

I commented that I was pleased to see how they had all gelled and seemed less cliquey than they had at the start. I was pleased they'd all had the opportunity to express themselves, raise any concerns and collectively find workable solutions to roadblocks. As I packed up my workshop tools and prepared to leave, Tom came over to thank me and shook my hand, quite vigorously, which felt very different to the first time we'd met. I believed that this time he meant it, and I sensed that he felt it, too.

One week later, I followed up the Team Strategy workshop by collating a report based on the outputs from the event, including some suggested next steps, such as recommendations for Tom to begin delegating out all of the various action points that had been raised, and to continue the conversations while, crucially, involving the whole team. As is my usual practice, I signed off by saying if there was anything else Tom felt he needed help with, he could feel free to get in touch. I suspected he probably would do just this, and my intuition proved to be correct. It was only a couple of days later that Tom called me, and that was what led to my journey to Cambridge on a blisteringly hot July day.

The present day

When Tom eventually breezed into the meeting room, ten minutes late, yes, he was checking his phone. Despite his tardiness and distraction, he seemed genuinely delighted that I'd responded to his email invitation by saying I'd be happy to have a face-to-face debrief and meeting.

After some pleasant small talk, we chatted about what I'd taken away from the Team Strategy workshop and I got straight to the point. First off, I needed his full attention, and would he mind switching off his phone, given his predilection for distraction and plate spinning?

'Of course, sure, no problem,' he said as he buzzed Ruth in and, to her obvious astonishment, asked her to take his phone and ensure we weren't disturbed, unless it was 'an utter emergency'. Ruth, as I then discovered, could raise one eyebrow in arched surprise. She looked at me as if I was some kind of sorceress and had cast a spell on Tom.

When we were finally alone, I had Tom's full attention. His demeanour towards me had definitely changed since our first more formal encounter when we were preparing for the workshop, and I could now tell he knew that he needed help – my help – when he had previously thought that a Team Strategy workshop would provide an instant solution as he set out his vision and the goals for the team. Instead, what the workshop actually did (as it was meant to) was to highlight that none of the company's problems could be fixed in one day. While there were some immediate benefits from the workshop, there was also some significant rebuilding needed.

The business and its problems had grown organically at a fast, exponential pace, but as it had lacked the right management structure and mindset for so long, to reverse these problems was like turning the *Titanic* at full speed. Tom's clients had always loved him, but they were becoming a little bit restless, mainly because they weren't getting the responses they needed or were used to from TBB. They were experiencing compliance issues where TBB hadn't delivered on time, due mainly to the fact that Tom was the bottleneck.

He seemed a little nervous as he poured me another coffee from the flask. He looked tired, and in a flash, this reminded me of when I was leading a large team in big pharma. I never seemed to find enough time for myself, either in the office, or more importantly at home. I wondered to myself how late he eventually got to bed last night and how little sleep he'd had, those last emails of the day preying on his mind, preventing him from fully switching off as he composed some reply, despite the fact his body was desperately telling him to get some sleep. When you're the head or leader in a company, especially when you're newly propelled into that role, you're expected to take everything on and deal with matters you've never had to deal with before, and so I felt for him.

I myself have experienced the catapult from being a technical expert in one area to suddenly running a company where I had to understand everything from finance to human resources (HR) and health and safety. I found myself worrying about minutiae one minute – were there enough tea bags in the tea caddy? – then dealing with a major issue the next, while all the time juggling the needs of my clients. No two days ever seemed to be the same; there was always something new beyond my comfort zone that I had to somehow grapple with because of my newly elevated position.

Not long after my first anniversary as a senior leader, I joked with my colleague that it was the first day where I'd actually done something for the second time. By the time ten years had passed, it had become second nature, but right now, Tom was still new in his role as the CEO of a fifty-five-person company. He'd never intended to build such a business; he was a consultant who then needed increasing amounts of help as the business and his reputation grew. He started by hiring two people, then by the end of the first eighteen months, he'd hired three more. By year three, the company had grown to twenty people, which was when Tom decided to expand into his own offices as he began to consider how he could scale.

Until now, he'd not looked for any external investment, but over the last year, he'd really been struggling. His name had become synonymous with the business and he was still the signatory and the person carrying out many of the top-level tasks. He continued to write all the processes and held the strings tightly, but he was aware that all was not well. He personally felt out of control, his inbox was overflowing, and all roads led to Tom.

He'd created a trap for himself. So deeply ingrained was his connection and, dare I say, obsession with his business, he didn't trust anybody else to do things right. Everything had to channel through him. His core problem was not having the capacity to manage that as a strategy. The load had eased somewhat in that he now had an office manager, a finance team and some senior managers who reported directly into him, but he was still struggling to fulfil his role as CEO. He knew there were shortcomings in his systems and procedures, but he wasn't sure why or how to correct them, or how he could get his team to gel in the way they did during the workshop.

The clique

I commented that his team was transformed during the workshop, from a disparate group of individuals into a group that could work together. Tom nodded thoughtfully and admitted he'd been both surprised and excited by what he'd noticed. He completely agreed that he had a tendency to surround himself with a small clique of trusted individuals, but he didn't know what to do about it.

Tom then told me he could really see how the workshop had shone a light on the team as a whole, many of whom he'd never had any meaningful contact with before. Usually, when he arrived at work, he'd head straight for his office, breezing briskly past workstations, not acknowledging anyone apart from his longest serving colleagues: David, head of consulting, and Rachel, head of projects. If he was feeling up to it, he might include Chris, head of business development, but no one else, so the workshop had come as a complete shock to him in realising that his go-to guys, David and Rachel, weren't the only ones who knew about the business. Anybody could contribute ideas and opinions that were worth paying attention to.

It also hadn't escaped his attention that both David and Rachel had begun the workshop day clearly feeling out of their comfort zone, and perhaps that was down to the anticipation of Tom actively listening to and engaging with others apart from them. They might even have felt slightly jealous that they weren't the only ones who had Tom's ear. Their body language had said it all – crossed arms, grumpy expressions, downward looks, low energy postures, along with the inevitable barbed comments. It was obvious they resented other people generating new ideas, offering insights into systems and procedures that they felt were irrelevant, and having to sit through a workshop led by an outsider.

The clique Tom had helped create was an uncomfortable reality. While he intuitively knew that the team dynamic wasn't working, he felt that being pals with just a handful of his colleagues was an effective way of getting them on board. In truth, the workshop had revealed that he was in fact alienating everyone else. That had never been his intention, but he'd only ever been the technical lead before founding TBB, and not a leader of people. He had nothing else to measure his experience by.

Keeping the momentum going

Tom told me that as the workshop had continued into the afternoon, he couldn't quite believe what he was seeing and hearing as David and Rachel, and the always ebullient Chris, let their barriers drop, opened up to listen to the rest of the team, and at times, even agreed with their new ideas. It might even have come as a bit of a relief to them to realise that the pressure of being the self-nominated sole generators of ideas in the business was an artificial construct that had come about because the business had no mechanisms or processes to facilitate the collective consensus.

From my perspective, I had enormous sympathy with both David and Rachel because, without a doubt, they were the top performers in the business, but in holistic terms, they were at the bottom of the pile. I'd observed them being arrogant, dismissive and even rude to their colleagues. The fact they were part of a clique didn't make them a team. For so long, they'd 'got away with it' because Tom didn't want to rock the boat. He'd had no complaints as far as their deliverability was concerned, and most of the time, he was oblivious to their behaviours. They were great with their clients, and their numbers reflected that, but more importantly, Tom needed them because their inputs and outputs kept the company afloat. They were the centre of Tom's universe, and he was the sun around which they orbited in a skewed alignment – a fact that was now not lost on him.

What had interested me during our pre-workshop planning sessions was Tom reassuring me that he wanted my workshop to be part of ongoing development of both his team and the company, and himself. He was still surprised how David and Rachel had initially behaved towards me as an external person, and because he'd never seen his whole team operate as one unit before. He was eager to learn how to keep that momentum going.

Before I answered, I asked him to explain the management structure. In response, he drew a simple organisation chart. Considering Tom was someone who wanted to control so much of the business, I was surprised to see it showed various heads of department.

'Does each group head have the authority for that part of the business?' I asked.

'Yeah... but most, if not all decisions need to go through me.'

'How does that feel, with you as the linchpin?'

Tom paused for what seemed an age and it was clear this was a difficult question to answer.

'You've transitioned from a being a technical lead, where you were master of your own destiny in your own specific area, to being the boss of all these people,' I remarked. 'How does that feel?'

For the first time, he couldn't look me in the eye. 'It's harder than I thought,' he said. Almost immediately, he flushed with anger. 'I know it's a harsh thing to say, but people can be so annoying!'

'In what way?'

'I don't understand why people aren't more committed. We have so much to do and so many client deadlines to meet yet come 6pm this place is a graveyard.'

'Why would you expect the same level of commitment from your staff that you have as the owner of the company?'

I wasn't sure if anybody had ever directly challenged Tom on one of his core workplace beliefs before, but he was certainly a little taken aback. He realised I wasn't being combative, simply curious, and perhaps he was a little curious now himself.

'What's the culture here?' I asked.

This genuinely caught him off guard, and he looked at me blankly.

'What culture? We're just here, getting a job done.'

This is an aspect of company 'culture' I see quite often. When the leader occupies a client-facing role, they can be, as a result, unaware of what the overarching business culture actually is. In Tom's case, his two senior consultants, Rachel and David, worked solely with one client, and five other team members worked solely with another. The culture in TBB was to treat each team as if they were separate independent contractors who happened to sit in the same office together. I've seen this in large organisations, too, where the leader is so busy being involved in the process or project that they work alongside their colleagues independently, in many ways as a working group rather than as a cohesive team.

When I told Tom that was how I saw his business culture, I could tell he was feeling more and more lost. The realisation was dawning on him that he was a million miles away from having an engaged, unified team. When I noticed that look on his face, I filled in the pause quickly so he wasn't dwelling on that desperately lonely place.

'Do you want me to share how I think I could help?'

I know exactly what that moment feels like when someone offers help. It doesn't often happen to a leader, no matter what industry sector they're in. I know it can feel dreadfully lonely at the top. That's why I really felt for Tom, but with his insistent practice of writing all processes and being the chief conduit through which everything needed to be signed off while trying to be best mates with the top performers, who themselves were behaving pretty badly, he wasn't helping himself.

Tom's change of heart

It was evident to me that Tom was potentially the root cause of many, if not all, of the problems his business was facing, because he lacked the knowledge of how to be a leader. While his heart was in the right place, his head needed work, but I was confident that Tom would open up to the idea of taking the next steps towards leadership, with my help. As I started to explain my thoughts, I could see Tom visibly relax and fully engage with me. This was definitely a different Tom.

With that in mind, I explained that there was much work to be done, but it was all doable as long as he agreed to involve more people across the company. Although TBB was his baby, it was also now a business, and he needed to allow his colleagues to feel that they, too, belonged and hadn't just turned up to Tom's party. The sense of ownership needed to be more widely shared so that anyone who worked there could feel like they had a vested interest. The best way to make sure any employee cares about a business and its vision is to include them in the conversations, asking them, 'How are we going to get there?' Tom agreed with this, and in doing so, he turned a corner.

Our meeting ended with me having gained much insight and clarity as to why Tom needed my help. But while Tom had struggled, this didn't mean he wasn't able to succeed in his role.

When a business such as TBB focuses too much on delivering its products or services without concurrently building the leadership and structure, what often happens is that people develop reactive behaviours such as trying to maintain rigid control. All this does is burden the leader with more and more responsibility. They fear that if they loosen their grip, their control will slip and they risk upsetting or alienating both employees and clients, so their only course of action is to 'keep control, keep control, keep control'.

In spite of the company's current issues and challenges, Tom's creation of TBB was still a fantastic achievement. The most challenging aspect for Tom right now was that the business involved a huge amount of time and effort to control it, as well as ensuring it continually delivered. My initial thought was that we needed to look at how he could maintain that level of control while significantly delegating processes and tasks to other people, meaning he could actually have a bit of a life as well.

At this point, Ruth poked her head around the door.

'Sorry to interrupt, Tom, but you've got your next meeting.'

Tom looked up in complete surprise, and then glanced at his watch. He'd completely lost track of time.

'It's not a problem,' I told him, adding that I'd send through a plan as to how we could work together and delve more deeply into some of the items we'd already discussed. I'd also send him a draft of my methodology, which I'd explain to him in detail when we next met. Without thinking, Tom immediately suggested the same time next week and Ruth confirmed that she'd diarise this straight away. Again, Tom shook my hand vigorously and apologised for having to rush off, and we said our goodbyes.

Outside in the car park, the heat hit me as I left the cool air-conditioned offices. The temperature had risen to 33°C, but that's not what was on my mind. As I set off, I was already thinking about my next meeting with Tom.

Summary

In this chapter, we have already seen the stirrings of change in Tom's approach to his leadership of TBB, and in the way his teams interact with each other. Often the first step towards positive change is simply admitting that there is a problem.

To summarise, let's look at how Tom's journey so far ties in with the five pillars of the Leadership Vaccine:

- **Culture:** Tom learns that he needs a more open culture, not one that encourages cliques. Currently his teams are working in silos, so he needs to give everyone the opportunity to be heard, and in return their engagement with his company will grow. They need to be able to own both the direction the company is going in and their own roles within that direction, and to enable this to happen, Tom has to listen to each and every one of them and act on their feedback, even if it's only to explain why an idea won't currently work.

- **Scope:** Rachel and David, and to a certain extent Chris, are currently overstepping the boundaries of their roles, theirs being the only voices Tom has been listening to. As a result, the rest of his teams have been feeling it's beyond the scope of their roles to offer any suggestions. When this all changes during the Team Strategy day, the staff who had been ignored demonstrate that they have the experience to offer valid suggestions that Tom and his clique haven't previously considered, surprising everyone, especially Tom.

- **Structure:** Tom wants to take TBB to the next level, but has to face up to the uncomfortable truth that currently, he doesn't have the right structures in place to build a resilient business and to attract the investment he will need.

- **Staff development:** I encourage Tom to delegate the valid action points his team suggested at the Strategy day and continue to have conversations with all his staff, making sure everyone has a sense of ownership of future developments. Tom also needs to develop his own behaviours, starting with making sure he is fully present at all meetings, not distracted by his phone or the day-to-day running of the business.

- **Processes:** Tom realises he needs to delegate, while still maintaining ultimate control of the company's processes. He also learns that he needs to put in place processes to facilitate the collective consensus.

TWO
Leadership Blind Spots

2 August

I was on my way back to meet with Tom in Cambridge, travelling north on the now familiar route along the M11. Over the last seven days since we'd last met, I'd spent quite some time thinking about what I'd observed of Tom and his colleagues during the Team Strategy workshop and, more importantly, during my post-workshop meeting with him when I'd had the benefit of Tom's full attention, and he mine. I'd reflected on how he'd begun to open up – not to me, but to himself – about his worries and concerns that the business could stagnate at any point in the future and him not knowing what to do to prevent that. Instinctively, Tom knew he needed to make some changes, but instinct alone wasn't enough.

Just as Ruth was pouring my tea, Tom rocked up, ten minutes late as usual. Once again, he greeted me warmly, even though he soon got distracted by a 'Sorry, it's urgent' message on his phone. It was only 9.10 am and already Tom's day seemed to be getting off to a hectic start.

Emergency dealt with, he looked at me, apology written all over his features. It was almost as if he were admitting he was an addict wanting to kick the habit, so I gave him a head start.

'Tom, you know what I'm going to ask, don't you?'

'My phone,' he said, a little sheepishly.

I nodded, adding, 'If this is going to work today, then this meeting has to be a priority.'

'Sure, of course,' he said, immediately switching it off, although I'm sure it was causing him some pain to do that so early in the working day.

'I know what it's like. I understand you've got a million and one things going on. But I need your commitment that when we have meetings from now on, you'll be here on time and be present not just physically, but mentally too.'

'I know, I know, the last thing I want to do is waste your time. I'll do better, I promise.'

'That's all well and good, Tom, but trust me, words alone won't cut it from now on. This is a partnership here; I can't come in and just fix things for you. I don't have a magic wand. We need to work together on this. We only have an hour today, and we're already fifteen minutes in. And if nothing else, not being available to anyone else for an hour means you can just focus on one thing: you.'

'You don't beat about the bush, do you, Rebecca?' he said with a smile crossing his face.

'I see how much you want your business to work and I am absolutely committed to getting you there, but to really help you succeed, I need to say and do what I think is right for you and the business, even if at times it's not the most popular thing you'd want to hear.'

I registered his surprise. Clearly nobody had ever spoken to Tom like that – not at work, at least – but I think he welcomed my straight talking. To prove he'd not only listened but also taken it all on board, he snapped his phone cover shut and pushed it across the table towards me.

'Look, there you go. You know what? That feels really good. A little odd, I admit – I never switch my phone off.'

Just at that moment, Ruth knocked on the door and popped her head around it, but before she could say anything, Tom was quick to cut her off.

'Good timing, Ruth. Tell anyone who calls I'll get back to them later today.'

'What if it's urgent?'

'Only if it's a real emergency. Like the roof's on fire. Otherwise, make something up, cover for me – I don't know. Tell them I'm at the dentist, or that the dog's dead. Anything. It can wait till I'm ready, OK?'

'So, no calls? No signatures?'

'And no interruptions before ten o'clock.'

By the look on her face, Ruth now firmly believed I had a magic wand. Her eyebrow arching to new heights, she closed the door.

'I'm all ears,' Tom said.

It was important that I didn't immediately roll out a series of bullet points; I was saving those for later. There would be no point in laying out my thoughts about TBB's structure until I was happy that its leader was confident. I needed Tom to spend a little more time thinking about himself first.

Staff interactions

Leaning back in my chair, I asked, 'So, tell me, how are you feeling about all this? I mean, the business in general?'

'Like what?'

'Well, when you get out of your car and walk into the building, does your heart feel kind of heavy? Does it sink at the thought of something you know you have to do today that, if you're honest, you hate?'

Tom suddenly laughed and mirrored my pose, leaning back in his own chair. 'That describes most days! Where do you want me to start?'

'Exactly my point. But I bet nobody here's ever asked you how you feel about it, have they?'

'No. Why would they?'

'You can hardly blame them for that. After all, you are the boss. You're the one with all the answers, in their eyes.'

'So I'm told.'

'Do you enjoy it? Being in this leadership role?'

Tom looked away for what seemed an age as he considered the question. Eventually, he responded.

'It's my job, isn't it?'

But his body language and demeanour told me more about what he was feeling than his words.

'It's your job, yes, but when you look at leadership, what are the bits of it that you really enjoy?'

'That's easy. I enjoy strategising for the new projects, keeping an eye on them to make sure they are on track and that the processes are working, and ultimately that our clients have what they need.'

'What about the people aspect of leadership? Do you enjoy that?'

He shook his head. 'They don't really need me. I just sit in my office and get on with stuff, my stuff. They look after themselves and only see me if there's a problem.'

When I asked who he would generally speak to in the course of a day, he mentioned Rachel, David and Chris, and occasionally Sophie who handles finance. Out of a company numbering fifty-five, this isn't a big number, but Tom was quick to point out that he'd have team meetings with his other direct reports, Jake and Sandeep, from time to time, and that they'd also have meetings with their own people, as and when required.

'Besides,' he pointed out, 'everyone talks to each other the whole time, even if informally so, and because it isn't a big office, there's little need for too many meetings, let alone one-to-ones. As long as they do what they need to do with the projects, I let them just get on with it.'

'Based on the processes that you write? And they follow?'

'Yes.'

'What about reviews? Do you monitor their personal-development plans, how much progress they're making?'

'I only review things when I know something's not working properly within the process.'

'So, when mistakes happen?'

'If you want to put it like that, yes.'

'How often would you meet with your teams outside of those types of situations?'

'That's easy to answer – I meet them for a client over-sight meeting, or when we have a senior management get together. Or for any project review meeting.'

'How often would that be?'

'Whenever I think it's needed. Say, when we're develop-ing a new project strategy, I'm generally leading that.'

'Would I be right in saying, then, that most of your staff interactions arise when it comes to discussing projects, and that you're always the one leading those conversations?'

'Probably.'

'So, you never initiate one-to-one meetings, and you've never really held a team meeting where its purpose has been to see if your direction is heading the right way? Or just to see how people are getting along?'

Tom shuffled in his seat, probably hoping that Ruth would burst in to say the roof had caught fire after all.

'No,' he said simply.

'Good,' I said, beaming, 'now we're getting somewhere.'

'Really?'

'Yes, because it's obvious to me that all of your inter-actions are very much rhymed to the work, and to the processes that you've created and instilled into everyone. I'm not judging you for that, Tom, I'm just saying it like it is. I get it, I understand, especially when there's nobody to ask you how you feel about things.'

'I'm not the touchy feely type.'

'But you're obviously a nice guy. I'm sure you'd only have to ask your clients to know that. Look where being you has got you already. But being a leader isn't simply about being you anymore, is it? It's more than just people following processes that you've set down for them, and then you checking up to see if they're doing their jobs properly.'

'What would you suggest?'

'To start with, I'd like you to get to a point where you have regular one-to-ones. I don't mean with everyone in the company, but with your senior management and team leaders. Then hold more team meetings and set the direction that you want the business to go in. Just think back to the Team Strategy day to see how many of your people who never normally speak up want to feel included and be part of the business direction.'

'Yes, I admit, that surprised me.'

'I'd also like you to get to the point where you can offer the time and resources to help your people develop their own skills and confidence, so they can actually begin to write and manage all those processes that you currently create for them. At the moment, you're still occupying the role of a subject-matter expert as if you were in a large corporate organisation. But like it or not, Tom, this time, you're the leader. People look up to you for more than just your expertise and knowledge in your subject area. That's what we need to work on so that you can get the best out of your people, and yourself.'

'Wow! That's not where I thought this would go.' As Tom spoke, it was clear he was ticking over all I'd said in his mind. 'I initially thought you'd come in and help me sort out my teams and their project delivery issues. I'll be honest, I just don't understand why they're not doing what I'm telling them to do. The processes are clear and I've written them in such a way as to be easily followed. I've even trained everybody on them, so that's why I don't understand why they're falling behind.'

I felt for his misguided perception of what makes a leader effective. After all, if he'd never had any real experience or training in leadership, the picture could easily be blurred and influenced by the role models he might have had in the past.

'You've never actually had to lead a team of people before?' I asked.

'No. I've only ever been a technical leader. As you said, a subject-matter expert responsible for leading matrix teams, and then bringing the project team together. One-to-ones or team meetings never happened because there was no need, since nobody reported directly in to me.'

This confirmed what I'd been thinking. Tom lacked real awareness of his people and their need for development, wellbeing and empowerment within the business. These were concepts completely outside of his direct experience, so it was little wonder that he was struggling to manage them now that the business had grown beyond a handful of consultants.

A revealing tour of the office

This was my second site visit and I was aware that I'd not seen any of Tom's teams in action, so I asked if he could give me a tour. Moments later, we were on the fourth floor and walking through the office. Within seconds, a regulatory assistant, Tamika, grabbed Tom's attention, looking for an answer to a particular problem with a project scoping document for a client. I made it clear to Tom it was OK to divert his attention away from our meeting as this would provide valuable insight for me.

Tom launched into the nitty-gritty detail of the process with Tamika and dictated the body of the email, along with the instruction to let him check it first before she sent it to the client. What interested me was that Tom made no attempt to ask for Tamika's thoughts, or offer any sort of guidance that would help her in the future.

I'd also noticed that when Tom walked through the office, he didn't engage with anybody, unless they spoke directly to him, as Tamika had. There were no calls of 'Good morning', 'Hi, how are you?' or anything personal between him and his staff.

Tom's office was nearest to the door. After he'd finished with Tamika, I asked him how often he walked through the main office as we were doing now.

'I don't. Generally, I just head straight to my office.'

Engagement was certainly not a top priority, but notwithstanding this, as the boss of the business, while Tom may not have noticed his people, they certainly noticed him. Many of them, particularly those who hadn't been part of the Team Strategy day, were now straightening up in their chairs, looking industrious on calls or emails. For his part, Tom was oblivious that he'd had any such effect on them whatsoever.

When we sat down in his office after the walkabout, he was genuinely taken aback to hear that he seemed to come across as an imposing and frightening figure. He was 'Just Tom', wasn't he? If anything, he believed he felt more worried by people than they felt by him.

Tom got up and closed the door to his office. It was surprisingly quiet in there when he'd done so.

'I had it designed and installed like this specifically,' he said proudly. To my mind, though, it simply underlined the division between him and his team members.

Summary

Gradually, Tom is becoming more aware of what is really lacking in his business, and why the work isn't getting done in the way he would like it done. Let's now relate what he's learned in this chapter to the five pillars of the Leadership Vaccine:

- **Culture:** Tom and I reflect on the fact that the culture, or lack thereof, in TBB has led to the teams rarely discussing their work with him – or anything else, for that matter – just as he has never asked for input from them when developing the processes they have to follow. The only time he really meets with the majority of his staff is when something has gone wrong, or to outline a new project where he simply instructs them on how it will be rolled out. As we walk through the open-plan office on the fourth floor, I'm dismayed to notice that Tom only engages with his staff if they first approach him; he makes no attempt to offer them a greeting. For their part, though, the staff certainly notice him, becoming extra industrious as soon as he enters the room. This reflects an old-fashioned hierarchical culture of fear rather than a far more effective culture of shared responsibility.

- **Scope:** Tom reveals that there are many aspects of his job that he doesn't enjoy at all. He and I then discuss what he feels his role is now, and I urge him to look more at what it should be, rather than only focusing on the parts of the business he enjoys.

- **Structure:** Tom starts to understand that the structure of the business has to originate from him as business leader, but currently he is behaving like a technical leader who would have no need to implement the structures required to run a successful business.

- **Staff development:** I recommend that Tom start with himself, developing the skills he needs as a leader rather than the subject-matter expert he once was. He needs to change his mindset on the processes, too, realising that people want to own their roles rather than being given a set of clearly laid-out instructions to follow, written by Tom with no input from anyone else. He also needs to recognise his people and their need for development, wellbeing and empowerment within the business.

- **Processes:** we discuss the fact that Tom has been leaving his staff to get on with things, following the processes he has written without consultation with them. He feels that as it's a small office, people will discuss problems informally, so there's no need for one-to-ones. He currently only meets with his direct reports, mainly Rachel, David and Chris. I suggest that Tom starts to communicate more with his senior management by implementing regular one-to-ones and really listening to their feedback. He's to follow this with more team meetings, allowing new voices to be heard as they were at the Team Strategy day. Then he needs to develop his people to the point where they can actually write their own processes.

THREE

Value

Before pressing Tom about some of the people on his team, I wanted to know his impressions of them and to work out if there was any correlation between these and his leadership approach. He began by singling out head of business development, Chris.

'Chris's great.' Tom said. 'He knows exactly what he's doing and he's on top of stuff. And he's really organised...'

This is when I sensed the 'but', and I wasn't wrong.

'But he drives me absolutely insane, because he is so...'

Tom seemed lost for words, a little exasperated by the very thought of Chris until he semi-exploded.

'He spends so much time on fluff! He always wants team meetings and initiatives that he'd been used to at the company I head hunted him from. He still doesn't get it – we're a *small* concern and we haven't got the time for all that personal-development shi... nonsense. Mind you, it was Chris who asked for the Team Strategy day.'

'So, he's got something going for him, then?' I laughed, and so did Tom, but it soon disappeared into a frown again.

'It's just that when he's in meetings, he talks nonstop.'

'Is that a problem? I mean, is that a problem for you?'

'Yes. I mean, no. I mean... I'll go to a meeting and say only what I need to say. There's no need to keep talking through everything, and by God, he talks. And then he just takes over the whole damned meeting.'

'In what way? How does he take it over, in your opinion?'

'Chris always wants to look at the bigger picture and never the detail.'

'And you love detail.'

'Yes, don't we all? That's where the Devil lives. Also, don't forget my time is pressed. I just want to do the work. Not this big-picture blue-sky-thinking crap. We've all got clear objectives.'

'Set by you?'

'Clear objectives, set by me, yes, which we all need to do, and that means we need to follow the processes so we can deliver to our clients. Simple. I don't understand why we always need to take this "let's step back" view he always drones on about. Urrgh! And to be honest, I don't really want to get rid of him...'

'You've actually thought about firing him?'

'No, not at all.'

'Why not?'

'Because he's integral to what we do.'

'What would the business be like without Chris? What's it like when he goes on holiday, for example?'

'There's the thing. It's not the same, and I actually find it quite stressful because I know he's got most things covered when he's here, and then when he's not, I don't have a clue. But jeez, the days he calls in sick are the days that I love the most and I can really relax. I'm guessing you're going to tell me that's wrong of me?'

It was obvious that Tom recognised Chris's core value, even if he couldn't truly identify what that value represented. All he could focus on was Chris's personality, which was so different to his own.

'If only he could put all that fluffy talkative energy into the detail.' As if to prove his point, Tom suddenly seemed drained. 'I find that to be around Chris is absolutely exhausting. Often, we just don't see eye to eye. Which is fine, I guess, for the most part, especially as people tend to go to Chris with their questions or problems, rather than coming to me. In fact, thinking about it, that suits me fine. Leave me to get on with my own stuff. I don't need to know all the nitty-gritty details of people's lives. I've got a job to do.'

Therein lay much of Tom's problem. He was a doer who'd never spent time thinking about the culture of the workplace he'd created as his business grew.

Abdication over delegation

From what I'd seen of Tom, practically everything he was assuming responsibility for, he could, in fact, delegate. Instead, he was abdicating from his leadership responsibilities.

Let me explain what I mean by this. If we look at the responsibilities of a leader, we may have one-to-ones with team members, initiate development plans, encourage feedback, bring the team together and motivate them. A person in the role of a leader may also be a subject-matter expert for a process, lead projects, and be responsible for writing procedures, overseeing key performance indicators (KPIs), developing and running a budget. But what elements can be delegated and what do we need to hold on to? Many leaders I've spoken to would say they need to keep control of everything and also be the main subject-matter expert. I would argue that's not always the case.

What I was seeing with Tom, and what I so often see, was that while he was busy 'doing', one-to-ones and looking at development opportunities for his team were falling by the wayside. In spite of these being the things that only he as the leader could do. He didn't need to be the subject-matter expert; he didn't need to write all the procedures. If he had trust in his teams and was developing them in the right way, he would be able to pass on key responsibilities while remaining accountable and comfortable in that space.

While Tom was the ultimate leader in TBB and had direct reports that he was responsible for, he was not carrying out any of his leadership responsibilities. Nobody in the business, it seemed, could articulate any real sense of what the company vision and values were, least of all Tom. At TBB, staff were currently turning to Chris with their problems, be they personal or work related, when the person they should have been turning to was Tom.

I did see that Tom was the technical leader. On that basis, I asked him, 'Is this technical leadership quality something that you can develop to become a business leader, or would you prefer to step aside and allow somebody else to take over that role?'

'You mean, like Chris?' he asked me, shocked. I reminded him that he wasn't actually carrying out any of the line manager roles himself, so by default, Chris had fallen naturally into this. Tom's disengagement with the 'fluff' had got Chris on first name terms with all the employees, a responsibility Tom had happily and passively abdicated because he didn't value it.

'Tom, it's not all about you,' I reminded him.

This wasn't just a case of Tom being too busy to lead. When I scratched below the surface, I saw he was actually leading in the manner he'd like to be led. He liked to be told what to do and left alone to get on with it; he found talk of vision too non-specific, people interactions too uncomfortable (and, to some extent, unnecessary). He liked to be able to consider options and confirm them over email rather than having more discursive brainstorming meetings, where ideas and concepts could crop up out of nowhere.

It is at times like this when the personality preferences of the people we work with are so important to understand. Each of us has our own preference in how we communicate, make decisions, like to manage and react to stress. Just because Tom had certain likes/dislikes/

needs didn't mean that they applied to everyone else in his business. It was great that he seemed clear on his own likes and how he wanted to operate, but there appeared to be no self-awareness of how this impacted on those around him, combined with a lack of empathy towards other people's possibly opposing preferences.

When it came to Chris, I realised from what Tom had told me and from what I'd observed during the Team Strategy workshop that he and Tom had personalities that, although very different, could be complementary. Chris liked being around people much of the day; Tom preferred the comfort of his sound-proofed office. Chris loved to talk through ideas; Tom preferred to have time to consider and reflect. Chris looked at the bigger picture; Tom loved the detail. This could be a marriage made in heaven, or it could be the partnership from hell if neither understood their personality preferences.

Personality preferences

Carl Jung first described personality preferences in his 1921 book *Psychological Types* where he discussed how we each have four basic mental functions.[2] When fully developed, these allow us to operate at our best.

---

2   C Jung, *Psychological Types* (Routledge, 2017)

1. Perceiving – how we take in information

Two of Jung's mental functions relate to how we perceive the world and take in information – these are sensation and intuition.

Those with a preference for the former (sensation) are those focused on the here and now, the detail, the facts. They rely on past (direct) experience and value the accuracy of the data and information being presented.

Those with a preference for the latter (intuition) are the big-picture thinkers who like to look for patterns, meanings, connections and at the wider context. They enjoy a degree of ambiguity, seeing this as opportunity, and rely on ideas and inspiration. By this point, you can probably guess where Tom and Chris sat and why they didn't always see eye to eye.

These differences can indeed divide us but having both preferences in the management team can be absolute magic. Let me explain with a little analogy.

Imagine a couple, one with an intuition preference (let's call him Ian) and the other with a sensation preference (Sam) who are planning on buying a house together. They arrive at a viewing for what they hope will be their dream home. On entering the property for the first time, Sam sees there's a lot of work to be done due to the run-down state. She sees the cracks in the walls, the rattling radiators, the old light fittings – a stark reminder of their flat ten years ago when they were first time buyers.

Ian, on the other hand, has already sorted the room allocations. He's imagining the parties they'll throw, knows exactly where the Christmas tree will go, seeing far beyond the nuts and bolts.

Both Sam and Ian see the property as an opportunity to purchase, but they are each taking in the information presented to them in the viewing based on their different personality preferences. By bringing the two together – reality and detail and the benefit of past experience, and possibility and vision – they create something of potential beauty that embraces both sides of the story. They can see how this property could be their dream home and they're able to make the decision taking into account the cost and work required to achieve that dream.

When these differences are not leveraged, though, this can cause conflict with the result that the detail-oriented party feels that the big-picture visionary is unrealistic. Conversely, the big-picture thinker feels that their vision has been killed by the detail. I'd seen this in the interactions between Tom and Chris, and imagined it was being replicated across the organisation where the leader's (Tom's) focus was so strongly geared towards the detail without him being aware how this might have been turning those with opposing preferences off.

2. Judging – how we make decisions

Knowing how we perceive things, we then make decisions based on one of Jung's two other mental processes, thinking and feeling. Those with a thinking preference are guided by logic, cause and effect, and arrive at a judgement based on fact and what's in front of them. Those with a feeling preference are guided more by personal values that stem from an individual-based standpoint. This does not mean that people with a thinking preference don't have any feelings, and that those with a feeling preference aren't at all logical; its more that their initial drivers are different.

Tom and Chris are the epitome of these differences. Tom ensures everybody has what they need to carry out their tasks; Chris, on the other hand, is concerned with ensuring that everyone feels involved in the process on a day-to-day basis. Both have a valid approach, but their drivers are different.

THINKING AND FEELING PREFERENCES

A perfect example of the thinking and feeling preferences at play arose a couple of years back. Our son, Ethan – about six years old at the time – came running down the stairs to show me a toy. As he got to about five steps from the bottom of the staircase, he tripped, falling and landing face down on the toy in the hallway. He let out a blood curdling scream, resulting in both me and my husband running to his aid.

I immediately gathered him up and hugged him tight, my main focus on making him feel better. My husband cradled his face in his hands, checking if his teeth were OK and if he had split his lip. I was focused on his feelings, my husband on the more practical physical injuries. We both cared deeply for him and felt his pain, but how we approached this was different. On reflection, it was beautifully complementary.

It goes without saying that had my husband not been there, I would have checked Ethan's teeth and lip. Likewise, if my husband had been alone, he would have hugged him, but most likely we would each have had these as our second responses.

How we interact with the world around us

Once we understand Jung's four mental processes, to better understand ourselves and those around us, we must also have an awareness of how we all interact with the world through the two orientation preferences described by Jung – extroversion and introversion.

So often we hear extroversion being associated with chatty, confident people and introversion being associated with shy, quiet individuals, but these are misnomers. Introversion and extroversion have little to do with social confidence; they relate more to where we get our energy from – the external environment or our inner world of thoughts, reflections and feelings.

Let me explain this in the context of Chris and Tom. In meetings, Chris talks through his thoughts, likes to brainstorm ideas in the groups, enjoys active discussion, and will often let his mouth lead him. He seems to buzz from the energy of the room. Tom, on the other, hand likes to consider, reflect and gather his thoughts, thinking through ideas before sharing. Tom is not shy, and Chris is not particularly confident, but on the face of it, Chris's active sharing and Tom's reluctance to do so may point to this being so.

Every business needs all preferences

At this point, I hasten to note that I'm referring to personality preferences, which must not be confused with personality traits. Traits dictate performance, whereas personality preferences do not. Personality preferences are just that: preferences. We are all able to look at things and operate from both perspectives, but one will feel more natural.

For example, if we break our preferred hand, we can make do with using our other hand, but it's not as natural. However, after a while, with practice, it feels less uncomfortable and more normal. It's the same with personality preferences.

While personality preferences do not dictate performance, they do affect our energy levels. For example, when Chris talks about big-picture ideas in his usual forward-thinking way, Tom finds it really draining because it's not his preferred manner of looking at information. Tom takes energy from being in his office with the door closed, but that doesn't mean he can't step outside and play an active part in meetings. But when he's in a team situation, such as the Team Strategy day, as much as he enjoyed it and drew enormous value from it, it would have drained him completely, whereas Chris was buzzing and loved it. Chris is also an engineer by training and can comfortably sit with data and analyse the nitty gritty, but too much of this type of activity drains him, just as meetings drain Tom.

If they can both recognise these different preferences in themselves, this will lead to less judgement, and less internal and actual conflict. Instead of each finding certain situations stressful and avoiding them, they will fare better in the long term by telling themselves, 'It's possible, I can do this', despite finding it strenuous. Not only this, but by better understanding where those around them get their energy from, Tom and Chris will be able to ensure they are bringing other people along with them, leading them as they need to be led, rather than just how they as leaders like to lead.

Understanding more about himself and the people he's surrounded by on a daily basis is one of the tools Tom can immediately put to use by being mindful of his potential blind spots and actively accounting for them. I have assured Tom that leaders *can* be natural introverts, be detail oriented and make decisions based on logic. There is no ideal leadership profile. All personality preferences have strengths and blind spots.

To be a strong leader means bringing people along with him, making the best of his team's talents, ideas and resources, being self-aware of his own strengths and blind spots, while also having a degree of empathy and understanding of those who might have different drivers, needs and challenges. On that basis, at today's meeting, I recommended that Tom and his leadership team attend a Personality Assessment workshop.

'What on earth does that involve?' Tom asked, narrowing his eyes, intrigued by our discussion so far. I explained it's a one-day workshop that delves deep and explores team members' personality preferences.

'Does it work?' he quizzed me.

'Absolutely, and for leaders, it's invaluable.'

'Really?'

'Sure. Once you're aware of your personality preferences and what blind spots and strengths these bring, it allows you to be more mindful of how you communicate, make decisions, react to stress and lead your teams. Developing empathy allows you to recognise others' potentially opposing preferences and how in response you may sometimes act, or indeed react, in ways that don't serve your colleagues well.'

'Presumably, the other managers will learn more about me, too?'

'Absolutely. They'll understand why you operate better behind a closed door. It doesn't mean to say you're not all working towards the same aim, or that they're not welcome in your office.'

Tom fell into deep thought as we sat there in his silent office. Then he broke the silence, thinking his words through carefully.

'Do people think that they're not welcome in my office?'

'Perhaps. In the same way that some people might think that those who like to talk through ideas throughout a meeting are trying to take over.'

'Oh, I see what you are getting at!'

'Don't worry. With this understanding, there are simple things that we can say and do to show empathy and understanding with someone who displays a different personality preference to us. It's about finding that common ground. You're likely to be surprised how this will help your relationships with the people around you and how you feel about these interactions.'

Our hour was rapidly drawing to a close, and once again, we'd covered a lot of ground in a short space of time. Tom was beginning to understand that being a leader was loaded with layers, but once he could gain an understanding of other people's preferences, and not think of them as traits, he'd learn how to better communicate and engage with the rest of the world, for its benefit, and his, too.

A few weeks later

25 August

Tom, Chris and the rest of the management team joined me for the workshop I had recommended. Throughout the day, I'd planned exercises to explore preferences:

- Exercise 1 – Team 1 introverts; Team 2 extroverts

- Exercise 2 – Team 1 sensation types; Team 2 intuition types

- Exercise 3 – Team 1 thinkers; Team 2 feelers

The teams explored their own preference and fed back to their counterparts in the opposing teams. It was really powerful to hear each preference team member talk about how they liked to receive feedback, or how they looked at data or the environment they liked to work in. Tom and Chris spent much of the day on opposite sides of the room to each other, hearing each other explain their preference, showing how different their personalities were. It allowed them to see that it wasn't a case of a right or a wrong way of looking at things; it was just differences which, when put together, enriched the team's collective approach. Hearing how others liked to receive feedback really grounded Tom as he realised that by steering clear of anything other than formal end-of-year feedback (in the fear of appearing 'fluffy'), he'd risked demotivating other team members, a fact he'd never realised before.

The final exercise of the day focused on how the team members liked to prepare for a holiday – planning or spontaneous. All of a sudden, Chris and Tom were in the same group – both with a preference for detailed step-by-step planning. Other team members who held a preference for more spontaneity and keeping options open were on the other side of the room. Suddenly, Chris 'got' Tom and Tom 'got' Chris. Here they understood each other completely and were energised in their discussions on how they would go about their holiday planning. They laughed at how they were now sitting alone together, showing them that while they may have many differences, there is always common ground.

Later, Tom reflected on the day's events as he travelled home, sending me a text message:

'OK, so I get it. Goodness me, we are different – I mean that in a good way – and yet so similar as well! It was awesome to see how much strength we've got in this team when we all come together. Really excited to see how we are going to work together as we build TBB. See you in a few weeks – don't worry, I won't be late!'

I smiled as I read Tom's text, although one word stood out – a word I didn't think I'd heard from him at all in any of our first few meetings: 'together'. Change was happening. I could see the light at the end of the tunnel, which was just as well as it was time for us to approach the first pillar of The Leadership Vaccine – Culture.

Summary

We have spoken about the five pillars of The Leadership Vaccine and their importance in developing a high-performing team. However, before we can fully start to explore and implement these pillars, we must first build self-awareness of our own drivers, approaches and shortcomings and an appreciation and understanding of those of our colleagues if we are to be successful in creating meaningful and sustained change for our organisations. It is for this reason that this is the first of our Leadership Vaccine Tenets.[3]

Leadership Vaccine Tenet One:

VALUE your strengths, understand your blind spots and develop empathy for others.

By being more self-aware of our own personality preferences, we become more mindful of how we communicate, make

---

3   Turn to the Appendix to see The Leadership Vaccine illustration showing the how the tenets and pillars sit together.

decisions, react to stress and lead our teams. Developing empathy allows us to recognise others' potentially opposing preferences and how we may sometimes act, or indeed react, in ways that do not serve our colleagues well.

Tom and I discuss the concept of personality preferences, first introduced by Carl Jung almost a century ago, and how by ensuring that the business takes into account different preferences, team members' contributions can complement rather than conflict each other. Being aware of personality preferences will also enable Tom to connect with and receive feedback, suggestions and insights from all members of the team.

I highlight to Tom that an individual's personality preference does not determine their ability but rather how much energy an interaction requires. For this reason, individuals such as Tom, may find that they avoid certain situations. Due to Tom prioritising self-reflective, detailed activities over person-to-person interactions, open discussions and brainstorming, he and his team currently miss out on important development opportunities. I assure Tom that leaders *can* be natural introverts, be detail oriented and make decisions based on logic. There is no ideal leadership profile. All personality preferences have strengths and blind spots. At present, Tom's team members are turning to Chris with their problems rather than Tom as the leader. Although this suits Tom's personality preference as it frees him up to get on with his own tasks, it's not representative of a healthy team structure.

I encourage Tom to be mindful of his blind spots and actively account for them. At the Personality Assessment workshop that follows our conversation, Tom really has his eyes opened as he observes all the different preferences of his team members. He also sees how two people with apparently opposite preferences – himself and Chris – can still find common ground.

FOUR

Advocate Part One

One of the first things I noticed when I walked around TBB's office with Tom was that he didn't seem to know many people. There was no real sense of familiarity between him and his teams. In fact, team members had little or no personal interactions with Tom, or between themselves. It felt more like an old-fashioned factory where people sat at their stations, working diligently, but robotically.

Somewhat ironically, it was in a factory where culture was first defined. In his 1951 book, *The Changing Culture of a Factory*,[4] Elliott Jaques described the culture of an organisation as being 'its customary and traditional

---

4   E Jaques, *The Changing Culture of a Factory* (Routledge, 2001, reprinted edn)

way of thinking and doing of things, which is shared by a greater or lesser degree by all its members'. For me, I think of company culture at its most basic level, as the impression or feeling you get when you enter an office, either as a client, a consultant, or a new employee, and start to understand what's going on, how people operate and the direction of travel.

I liken it to when you visit somebody else's house for the first time. Even if it looks similar to yours (similar furniture, layout and belongings), it nevertheless has a different smell and feel compared to your own home. That's how I like to unpick what company culture is. Basically, it's a fingerprint that's unique to that company. Even though there may be many similarities with other companies, its culture makes it unique in terms of what it is, what it represents, and what kind of employer it is.

It's so important when we look at company culture to ask, 'How do we want people to feel?' But company culture isn't just about the 'fluff', as Tom put it; it reaches far beyond feelings and touches all that we do. It's who we are as a business, our purpose, our values, where we are going and how we are going to get there. That being said, how we feel is a great place to start.

Belonging versus fitting in

When we sense that different smell in someone else's house, it's as if our brain gives us a gentle alert: 'You don't belong here, this isn't home'. Depending on other factors in the environment – perhaps whether we know the owner of the house, whether the house appears safe, whether we are physically comfortable – this signal may be mild, only just enough for us to notice it, but not enough to warrant us feeling unwelcome. Or it could, coupled with other concerns, become uncomfortable enough for us to wish to leave.

It's no different in the workplace. There, a great culture allows us to do our best work and feel a real sense of belonging.

To feel a sense of belonging, the team at TBB needed to understand how decisions had been reached and, wherever possible, be involved in reaching these decisions, something that had never crossed Tom's mind as necessary in driving the company forward. What he had begun to realise since I'd been working with him was that he, alone, wasn't the company, and the company wasn't his. It was also Chris, Rachel, David and everyone else's workplace, too. He might have been the founder and was the CEO, but he was simply another member of the company. I was thrilled with his progress in this regard.

Building on the work that I described in Chapter Three (strengths and blind spots), TBB employees were beginning to form a deeper understanding of how and why each was different to the other. These insights were allowing them to collectively articulate the future of the company. They'd all been surprised to discover that culture doesn't need to be one sided, either extrovert or introvert, loud and fluffy or serious and stagnant. Company culture is the umbrella under which all these personality preferences come together to decide what to do to build the TBB of the future.

29 September

The next time I arrived at TBB, at midday, Tom was not only on time, he was the first to welcome me to the office. He buzzed Ruth for coffee, and seemed surprised when ten minutes later, Jack, a designer, walked in armed with the replacement flasks as Ruth was taking a lunch break. Tom couldn't recall her taking a lunch break before. We both smiled at the thought, but perhaps for different reasons.

Over coffee, I ran through the highlights of the Vaccine's culture pillar. There are many perspectives that form a company culture, and as we discussed them, the importance of having a clear framework that wasn't set by him alone dawned on Tom, since it would invite the team to question what it was that they were doing and how they behaved. The bedrock of a positive team culture allows people to feel that they belong and have a rightful part to play, irrespective of their personality type. It doesn't matter if they're not loud, or reflective, or that much into the detail. Tom was realising that TBB comprised of a multitude of personality types and perspectives under one roof, and yes, he needed each and every one of them.

Vision, mission and values

For an expanding organisation such as TBB which is looking to compete with larger, longer-established organisations, having a defined and socialised vision, mission and set of team values is vital to its continued growth. As a rule, I don't like to oversimplify matters, but when it comes to vision, mission and values, there's no better place to start than with straightforward dictionary definitions:

Vision – 'The ability to think about or plan the future with imagination or wisdom.'

Mission – 'An important assignment given to a person or group of people.'

Values – 'Principles or standards of behaviour; one's judgement of what is important in life.'
– Lexico[5]

I explained to Tom, 'A company's vision is a long-term view, a guiding light and inspiration with an endgame in mind. It's not just about what the company itself does

---

5   Lexico, www.lexico.com (2020)

day to day, its bigger than that. For example, despite being small, my own company has a vision that is nonetheless far reaching: "To change the way highly regulated industries operate". Everything that I do is steered towards that.

'A mission, on the other hand, is what a company does each and every day to get to that end goal. In my case, it's "To empower leaders to build *connection* to their people and purpose, to gain *clarity* on their roles and responsibilities, and to drive *commitment* to shared goals and aspirations", connection, clarity and commitment being my company values – the fundamental guiding principles that are most important to me in my work. I believe that if my team and I do that every day, ultimately we will change the way highly regulated industries operate.'

Tom was truly fascinated by these concepts as he could see the tangible benefits if he applied them to his own business. It was as if he was unpeeling the tight wrapping tape around his company and daring to look beneath the paper at the waiting gift inside, still not knowing quite what it was.

'If you have a clear view on where TBB's going, what forms its guiding light and inspiration, and you know what you're going to do every day to get there, you'll be better able to communicate this with the likes of Chris, David and Rachel, and everyone else, for that matter. For example, even during the recruitment process, candidates will understand what you stand for. If you can align all of your goals to that, you can use this as an anchor for your decision making.'

Tom, deep in thought, nodded his agreement. 'I get it. I can see the value in all of that. It's something I've not always been clear about, or, to be honest, even understood why I would want to go through that process.'

'I have to admit that if you had spoken to me let's say ten years ago, I would have been the first person to say that a mission statement is nothing more than something pretty to put on the wall, pop on a website. But then I started to lead teams that needed to influence, needed to partner with other teams, needed to drive change, needed to oversee, monitor and request information, time or resources from our colleagues or from our partners, and then I realised how important it is for a team to be able to articulate its purpose, value and place in the market. Really, it's like asking why people should listen to you? Why should they work with you or for you? Believe it or not, a mission statement allows you the space to lead – you have set a direction, and in doing so can take your hands off of the reins, knowing that people continue in the right direction without your constant involvement.'

'To me, it felt like it would be more pain than gain, but now I can see the other side of the coin,' Tom said. 'I can definitely see the advantages.'

'What in particular?'

'You said it would free me up for a start.'

'The good thing is, you won't need a finger in every single pie. You can trust the process, trust that you and the team are on the same page, and because the vision and mission are shared across the team, decisions will be easier.'

'Explain that bit to me again.'

'For example, when you prioritise a new project knowing you've only got a certain amount of resources, you can say, "Hang on a second, what's our guiding inspiration? What's our mission? What are we doing every day? Do we go with X or with Y?" That's really important to remember, because if you end up having to choose between something, say, David wants and something Rachel wants, you can say to one or the other, "Sorry, but we're going to go with this idea because this is compatible with our mission." Assuming everyone's on board with that journey, it'll be a hell of a lot easier for them to understand your decision making.

'It really increases engagement if people can understand why they're going in a certain direction and what it is that they're doing. Why take on more projects just for revenue's sake which don't align with your vision and mission? You end up being known as a "jack of all trades and master of none". Whereas, if you have a clear direction, the questions become easy: "Does that move us towards our vision? Is it aligned with our company values?" If you haven't defined what the company vision and values are, how can you have that discussion? How can you have that expectation of your team? Your business might be here to serve your clients, but when you're a leader, you're in a job to serve those that you lead too.'

'OK, so be honest, why weren't you keen on my first stab at a vision?' Tom asked me. 'What's wrong with "We provide strategic engineering consultancy services to the medical-device industry"? I thought it was quite good. Obviously not!' He let out an uncharacteristic guffaw.

'It's not inspirational enough. It doesn't make you stand out in the market; it just tells the world what you do. As I said for my company, I'm incredibly passionate about changing the way highly regulated industries operate. Why? Because the work that we do is important.'

'Why?'

'My vision for Etheo is driven by the fact that the people I work with operate in highly regulated, fast-paced industries and have important jobs to do. But they also have a life. My mission statement is so ingrained in my belief system that it drives what I do, so it needs to be an almost unattainable goal to keep me motivated, keep me striving. It also allows me to communicate to my clients why it is that I'll commit to working with them.

'I'm committed to working with you, Tom, to change the way you operate to make TBB a better place to work for you and your team. You've got some really talented people here, but you don't know what's going on in their personal lives. You don't know how difficult it is for them to come to the office every day. What if they're not inspired when they get here? What if they don't have fire in their belly? Then all this – your brilliant business that you've spent the last five years painstakingly building – will eventually fall apart.'

'Wow. Tell it like it is, Rebecca.'

'I did warn you. Look, Tom, I'm not judging you...'

'No, no, no, it's fine. I need to hear this. Carry on.'

'The way I look at it, the vision is the destination. If I put my destination – my vision – as Oxford Circus, London into Google Maps, then I can either go by car (and I'd still need to choose a route) or I can drive to the railway station and jump on the train. But if it's been agreed that I'll mainly travel by public transport, specifically by train, in my values, I'll know not to use the car or coach. I'll either walk, take a local bus or a taxi to the station, board the train – and I might even need to change trains – before taking the Victoria Line Tube to Oxford Circus. There's a framework that anyone can follow exercising a degree of choice, without the nitty-gritty detail such as "You must sit in the front carriage; you must always sit on the right; you must do this, or that".

'If you don't have a clear framework for where you're going and how you're going to behave, you'll end up dealing with conflict, inefficiencies and people going off in different directions. It's a vicious circle where everyone's waiting for the leader to say what they need to do. Not only that, you'll have difficulty retaining staff, as well as marketing who you are and telling your client what you do. If you don't know where you're going and why you're doing it, how can anyone turn up for work each day and give it any sense of purpose?'

'Is that why you think we're stuck?'

'Partly. When I asked David the other day, "What's your purpose? Why did you come into the office today?" he looked at me a bit blankly before telling me he was here to provide consultancy services.'

'That's what we do, isn't it?'

'Of course, but that's no reason to leap out of bed every morning. If he'd said, "Our mission is we want to support our clients in making things quicker, faster, cheaper", I could then have asked him, "Why? What's your vision?" and he could have said something along the lines of, "Because we believe that innovation will lead to better outcomes for the human race."'

'Wow. I like that!'

'Exactly. And it's very different to saying, "I've turned up today to write this email the way Tom told me to write it."'

Tom was stunned into silence. For the first time, it seemed this observation had really hit home.

'I had no idea,' was his simple response.

Creating a mission statement

THREE QUESTIONS

When looking at a team mission statement, as a framework, start by answering these three simple questions:

1. Who is it that you're serving? *Who are your customers? They might be outside the organisation, internal stakeholders, the end customer or your partners.*

2. What is the transformation you're looking to bring or make?

3. What is your approach?

When any business is looking at its company culture, vision, mission and values, I'm a passionate believer in embedding them so deeply that if the organisation was a stick of rock and cut down the middle, they'd be written there for all to see. To achieve that, they need to be developed *for* the team *by* the team. In TBB's case, that couldn't be just Tom, Chris, David and Rachel working as a small unit.

To Tom's credit, our earlier work on the Team Strategy day had set that train of thought in motion and he realised he needed the input of more than just a select noisy and visible few. His revelations about that day keep coming; not only had he entered the room with his own viewpoint, but so had everyone else because they'd all dealt with clients. They'd all dealt with new starters coming in and they'd all had dealings with the regulators. Each had joined TBB from different, but similar organisations, and they all had their own views on why TBB even existed. But until that day, most had never articulated those opinions because Tom had never given them the opportunity to do so.

During that day, he'd heard things that really excited him and made him – and everyone else in the room – realise that perhaps TBB *is* unique in the marketplace after all. The team started to feel like 'family', which was quite the opposite to the tick-box training days Tom was more familiar with in his previous corporate life. This felt more like he was connecting the dots.

How to motivate

I told Tom of a recent experience where I worked on an offsite strategy day with an organisation which had a number of different mission statements written for different parts of the business. Its problem was in finding one overall mission statement to encapsulate the lot.

As with TBB, I used the structure of my Team Strategy workshop, except this time involving thirty individuals from across the organisation, each representing a department, role or level of seniority. It was not practical or necessary to involve everyone in the company; as long as everyone was represented, that was sufficient.

The aim of the day was to elicit answers from each person to questions that purposely didn't mention the words vision, mission or values. Instead, I simply asked the team to ask themselves:

- What is the real impact the work of my role/team has had on the end customer during the past three years?

- What are the skills, experience and/or capabilities required to achieve this impact for our customers?

- What are the positive team behaviours we need to display to achieve this impact and to make best use of our skills, experience and capabilities?

The workshop was arranged in such a way that people could capture their personal responses before they heard from others so as not to be swayed. We then heard, from each person individually, all the wonderfully different and diverse perspectives. Using tools and exercises, we brought all the insights of those thirty people together into one overall shared answer for each of the first two questions. For the third, I put the answers on the wall, a separate card for each behaviour, and asked the team to vote. We collectively decided upon our top three behaviours.

We ended up with a really clear story on what the organisation brought to its end client, how it did that and how the teams wanted to behave. We had the bare bones of the vision, mission and values of the organisation as a whole. People knew how they slotted into the puzzle and what their own value and worth to the business was. It came back to the fundamental concepts of motivation. You can give somebody all the money in the world, but when they have fire in their belly to get up and do what they want to do, they are much more motivated.

With TBB, some team members dealt with SMEs while others dealt with large corporates. Some were offering ongoing consultancy, others providing direct one-offs, but their ultimate mission, purpose and reason for being had to be clear and aligned to a common vision. That in itself would be motivating.

EMPLOYEE MOTIVATION

Contrary to popular belief, high salaries, a posh workplace and, dare I say, even beer taps in the office will not ultimately motivate a team. Why? Because these are extrinsic motivating factors, and as humans we're inspired and motivated by something a lot more intrinsic.

This isn't a new theory; it has been around for decades, and yet we're still not listening! Back in the 1950s and 1960s, Frederick Herzberg studied employee motivation and found the things that motivate us are somewhat distinct from the things that have the potential to dissatisfy us.[6] He also noted that the opposite of job satisfaction isn't job dissatisfaction. Instead, it is *no* satisfaction. Likewise, the opposite of job dissatisfaction isn't satisfaction. It is simply no dissatisfaction.

The factors that have the potential to motivate us he called 'motivating factors'; those that have the potential to dissatisfy us he called 'hygiene factors'. What might not be surprising is that within hygiene factors sit company policies and procedures, because we all know that if we're dealing with cumbersome, tricky and downright rubbish policies and procedures, it's going to cause us dissatisfaction in our job. Then again, using slick, easy-to-use policies and procedures are not massively motivating, either. We're unlikely to be posting on social media about how great our policies are; we're more likely to say, 'Yeah, they're OK.' Hardly an enthusiastic response.

---

6   F Herzberg, 'One More Time – How do you motivate your employees?' *Harvard Business Review* (2003)

What might be surprising to learn is that within hygiene factors we find salary and work conditions. If they're wrong, they have the potential to dissatisfy, but if they're right, they're not going to motivate us. What is going to motivate us, what's in motivating factors, are things like achievement, growth, recognition and the work itself.

The takeaway is that if you want to motivate your staff, then stop focusing on the work conditions and the salary. Get those right, of course, but focus on giving people ownership of their work, empowering them within a safe space to try and fail so that they can grow. Give them inspiring, purpose-driven work.

What more as leaders can we do? In particular, what did I want Tom to do next to fulfil his role as a leader? As somebody who really cares about leaders, their confidence and happiness, and how they feel about leadership, I was excited to see Tom over the next few months working closely with his team. I would see him build on the different pillars that provide the foundations for his own leadership, and the business as a whole.

Over the next few chapters, I'll share more of Tom's story and how he steered a course and reset the balance where he no longer needed to monitor or take every phone call or make every decision. He involved his team and gave them to space to grow, try and fail, and ultimately achieve. As result, he saw his business become more resilient and created a legacy so that the business would remain secure should anything adverse happen to him. For the first time, Tom felt cared for himself and protected from the many pitfalls that would lie ahead.

I came at this as a leader who'd been in Tom's shoes. It's incredibly lonely and scary to sit where he was sitting. He was responsible not only for the livelihoods, but also the careers of the people around him, as well being legally responsible because of the regulations. Change felt at best uncomfortable, and at worst daunting and intimidating. My job was to show Tom that both he and his team had the capability to do this and take TBB into its next positive chapter.

Summary

Leadership Vaccine Tenet Two:

ADVOCATE for the right culture in your team.

Set direction and foster trust through the development of a team purpose, vision for the future and shared team values.

What is company culture? I tend to think of it as the impression or feeling we get when entering an office, either as a client, a consultant, or a new employee, and start to understand what's going on. In the workplace, a great culture allows us to do our best work and feel a real sense of belonging. To feel a sense of belonging, the team at TBB need to understand how decisions have been reached and, wherever possible, be involved in reaching these decisions.

The bedrock of a positive team culture allows people to feel that they belong and have a rightful part to play, irrespective of their personality type. For an expanding organisation looking to compete with larger ones, having a defined and socialised vision, mission and set of team values is vital to its continued growth. With this in mind, Tom and I look at the dictionary definitions of these three words:

> Vision – 'The ability to think about or plan the future with imagination or wisdom.'

> Mission – 'An important assignment given to a person or group of people.'

> Values – 'Principles or standards of behaviour; one's judgement of what is important in life.'
> – Lexico[7]

We then discuss the importance of a mission statement, and I point out to Tom that it's about letting people know why they should listen to him and work with or for him. Simply, a mission statement allows him the space to lead – he will have set a direction so people can continue in that direction without his constant

---

7   Lexico, www.lexico.com (2020)

involvement. Clearly defining the vision, mission and values of TBB and getting everyone in the company on board will enable him and his teams to make decisions far more easily.

FIVE

Advocate Part Two

L ooking back to the Team Strategy workshop I ran for TBB, I saw that it was becoming clearer to Tom that simply bringing all of his team members to one table wasn't the automatic path to finding a solution. Yes, it's vital to consult different perspectives and different areas of expertise and knowledge on a problem, but at the same time, we need to be mindful of team dynamics at play that can sometimes result in a team being less than the sum of its parts.

An observation I made on the TBB Strategy day was how Tom, Rachel and David were an obvious clique. Together, they might have seemed like a decision-making powerhouse, but in fact, the decisions I saw them making appeared to result from a syndrome referred to by Irving Janis in the early 1970s as 'group-think'.[8]

Groupthink

As far as the business went, Rachel and David had been closely associated with Tom for a while, and he in turn relied on them. In spite of David and Rachel's 'bad' behaviour towards the rest of the group on the Strategy day, I still observed Tom's desire to be part of this little gang. Watching them together, I witnessed all the classic signs of groupthink: a tightly knit team that on the surface looked solid and functional, but underneath lay a subconscious fear of one or more people upsetting the applecart.

In a typical groupthink setting, the people in the group get on with each other famously with a great sense of bonhomie, but the desire to maintain harmony within the group is prioritised over critical thinking. At the beginning of the Strategy day, Tom wasn't standing back and taking all the suggestions into considera-tion. Instead, he was happy to fall in with David and Rachel's flow, and they in turn appeared somewhat superior (in their eyes) to the other team members. Cue the classic recipe for groupthink:

---

8   Iyrse L Janis, 'Groupthink', *Psychology Today* (1971)

- A cohesive team (Tom, Rachel and David)

- Structural fault (insulation of the trio from the rest of the team)

- High-pressure environment (the Strategy day itself)

Groupthink can be a both powerful and negative force. When people self-censor their thoughts and shy away from any form of dissent, they end up talking as a collective rather than as themselves in a show of apparent harmony. This is highly counterproductive, certainly from the perspective of a leader who's looking to gain the best solutions to difficult problems where no team member feels isolated.

On TBB's Strategy day itself, it became clear where structural faults lay. Even though Tom, Rachel and David were only a group of three, I could see the groupthink dynamic at play. What was so powerful was when they were each asked to answer a question on their own first and only then share it with the whole group after everyone had captured their individual answers, we stopped seeing the groupthink team opinion. Now we heard David's opinion, then Rachel's and finally Tom's. To everyone's surprise, most of all Tom's, the trio's opinions weren't always aligned. And that was the whole point of the exercise: to acknowledge that within the group existed as yet unarticulated and diverse ideas.

In the context of this new understanding, Tom was realising that his own leadership skills had lacked the ability to cut through this counterproductive dynamic at play within his team because he was, in fact, part of the problem. The potential outcome, as far as Tom was concerned, exceeded his best expectations. He now saw that by breaking through group thinking, he'd have access to a greater flow of creative opinions, ideas and solutions than he could possibly have imagined.

For their part, David and Rachel were also exposed to listening to other team members' ideas that would never have been given any airtime or consideration before, and they too could see that there were valuable insights to be gained from others within the company. The 'aha' moments at the end of a Strategy day are always precious to me when team members realise that they've explored new and dynamic ways of working with each other in the future.

For Tom, this was indeed a revelation. A week later, when he and I were going through the workshop learning, he reflected, 'You know what? I didn't know there were so many different viewpoints between Rachel and David, let alone in the business as a whole. How could I have missed that?'

I knew exactly where he was coming from and offered him this thought. 'Yes, but this is your business and it should be led by you along with your team. I encourage you to delegate, but you must make sure not to abdicate your leadership.'

Tom was really taken aback, and his eyes widened. 'Is that what I'm doing?'

'Think about it. You're giving David and Rachel unspoken permission to steer the ship.' I explained to him the features and outcomes of groupthink, and then said, 'You can't blame David and Rachel, though. They don't actually realise what groupthink is. They think the rest of the teams don't get them, that everyone else is wrong and they're right. And you're the boss who's let them get away with that.'

'Is that what's holding me back, as a leader?'

'Probably, if I'm honest. And again, I'm not judging you. It happens if we end up leading when we least expect it.'

'My problem is that I have to trust Rachel and David – and I do – because they're my top performers. I don't want to rock the boat because they're delivering the numbers. But if I'm honest, they're not the numbers I need if I really want to scale.'

'If they're not open to external challenges and different people's opinions, you won't be able to adapt, and the business will eventually suffer. Continuously challenging the status quo internally is essential to your growth, because you'll certainly be challenged externally by others wanting to jump in and take your market share. That's a high price to pay for dinner in Abilene.'

'I'm sure I've never been there, but I guess you're about to tell me I have,' Tom said, laughing a little nervously.

'Don't worry, Tom, we've all been to Abilene as part of our leadership journey.'

'Even you?'

'Absolutely me! Let me explain.'

Dinner in Abilene

'It's a story that really resonates with me from a paper by Jerry B Harvey, "The Abilene Paradox: The management of agreement".[9]

'It's a hot afternoon in Texas and Jerry's sitting on a veranda with his wife and in-laws, sipping on some ice-cold lemonade. Everybody's happy. Suddenly, Jerry's father-in-law pipes up and suggests that the group head to Abilene for dinner. Jerry looks up and innocently wonders why on earth they would want

---

9   J B Harvey, 'The Abilene Paradox: The management of agreement', *Organizational Dynamics* (1988)

to do that? It's over 50 miles away and there's no air con in the car.

'Before he can speak, Jerry's wife chips in and says she thinks it's a great idea, asking Jerry if he agrees. Jerry, not wishing to disagree with the group, does agree, as does Jerry's mother-in-law, who announces she's not been to Abilene for absolutely ages and yes, they should go right now. With that, they all jump into the sweltering hot car, windows wide open, and off they toot to Abilene.'

'Are they mad?' asked Tom.

'Wait till you hear what happens next. A few hours later, they're all back at the house and the mother-in-law gripes along the lines of, "I don't even know why we went to Abilene." Slowly but surely, they all start chiming in with, "I only went because you wanted to go" and "I only went because *you* wanted to go", and last but not least, "I only went because *you* wanted to go". Of course, it soon dawns on them that not one of them actually wanted to go, but they'd all assumed the others did, and so they ended up going on a fool's errand to Abilene.'

'That *is* madness!' Tom said.

'It is, but it's not unlike what I can see happening at TBB. Let's say Rachel makes an assessment of a particular situation. It may not even be what she genuinely thinks, but she believes it's what you and David want to hear. David then agrees, although he's saying to himself, "That doesn't sound right", but he goes along with it to keep the peace. It leads to a complete lack of communication where no one ever gets to share their true beliefs or opinions. As a result, poor decisions are made based on a lack of collective input, despite other team members having strong opposing opinions. It's like building a house of cards, except when it all falls down, everyone gets angry and starts piping up, "I didn't want that anyway".'

'That's so true – I overheard Alex say to David that this was what he thought was going on a couple of weeks ago.'

'What happened to Alex?'

'He put his notice in.'

'Did you accept it?'

'Of course. No point in hanging on to dead wood.'

'Except now you may think differently. Maybe Alex did have a valid reason or opinion, but there was nowhere in the business for it to be heard. Or at least, that's how he perceived it.'

'Then he should have spoken up sooner.'

'Exactly my point, Tom. The culture in TBB doesn't yet allow for that to happen, and so the cycle repeats itself. If you perpetuate an environment where people don't want to speak up, where people don't know each other well enough and don't connect with each other, they're always going to be incorrect in their assessment of what other people think. It boils down to a lack of trust in the culture you've allowed to grow around you, and I just don't think that's you.'

'No, it's not. Frankly, I'm appalled that people might not trust me.'

'It's not you they don't trust – you're the all-powerful Tom, remember? The one with all the answers...'

'Oh God, I've just thought of something. Does that make me the mother-in-law in the Abilene story?'

'I don't know, does it? People need to connect, or they'll never fully trust what the others are thinking. Look at how you and Phil found a connection over Pink Floyd when I asked everyone on the workshop day to discuss something that makes them happy.'

'I know, that was a real surprise. There were quite a few surprises, actually, things I wasn't expecting to hear. But some of them were so interesting, it did make me realise that I don't know my colleagues half as well as I should.'

This was just the sort of connection I'd hoped that Tom would be making. More often than not, Tom would say things that he thought other people wanted to hear. The cycle completed itself when they repeated back to him what they thought he wanted them to say. It was a game of ping-pong where it was difficult to know who the stronger player was, and that's a pitfall many leaders fall into when building teams.

Because meetings are built in such a way, we often don't know what other people really think. Wherever we might see groupthink and the Abilene paradox, it's really important that the leader holds back their opinion until others have spoken, because it allows others present to offer their ideas, and the leader may actually gain new insights from this. It also prevents closing down other people's ideas. If a leader kicks off the meeting with their own opinions, and then invites responses, it's highly unlikely that people will disagree with them.

In my early days as a manager, I'd been in the situation where I received feedback – via HR, no less – that I didn't take others' ideas onboard. I was mortified.

'What? I always ask for people's ideas.'

But what I was actually doing was walking into a meeting as the leader, saying, 'Hi, guys, what I think is blah, blah, blah. Now what do you think?' In my head, I genuinely wanted to hear their opinions, but all they heard from me was 'I'm the boss and this is what I think. Now I'm going to ask you what you think, but actually I don't really care.' I *did* care, but that's not how I came across, so nobody would ever give me their real opinion. As a result, we'd spend a lot of our time going back and forth to Abilene.

Each person brings something different to the table, and in this day and age where resources are stretched tighter than ever, particularly in smaller businesses, leaders need to squeeze out every bit of insight and knowledge from every single corner. Anything that blocks the flow of information sharing, be that group-think, Abilene paradox or other under-the-radar negative team dynamics, can be hugely detrimental to a business. If eight out of ten cats don't speak up and say what they really think during meetings, that's an 80% loss of knowledge.

As leaders, we can all positively influence the outcomes of meetings. If we imagine TBB as a product-based (physical goods) business that only actually sells 20% of those goods, that would leave the remaining 80% gathering dust in the warehouse. That simply doesn't make sense. People are a leader's single biggest asset. In not getting the full 100% of insights from our people, we're not actually leveraging our best assets to their fullest extent.

I told Tom how I took the feedback on my leadership skills on board and adjusted my behaviour. The immediate benefit to me was that it devolved responsibility away from me always having to go first. During a typical day, I could be involved in up to fifteen back-to-back meetings, where I'd be running from room to room and, on occasion, on entering a room I couldn't even remember what each meeting was about. To be able walk in, take stock of what was going on and hear what people's views were before I reached a decision meant that I was making more sound choices because I was in the right frame of mind, I had the right information and I understood the context in which I was making that decision.

Since TBB had expanded, Tom had been under a huge amount of pressure. He was the archetypal accidental leader: at heart he was a technician, so during any technical conversation, it was incredibly difficult for him to hold back because he was under pressure and wanted to make decisions so that the job would get done. Who was going to disagree with him? Whenever he held a cross-functional meeting, he'd often refer to Rachel and David first, so nobody else felt safe to offer a differing opinion.

Tom should be able to sit back, hear the discussion and listen to the expertise in front of him that he'd hired to find the solutions. He needed only to be accountable for steering the ship, but for so long now, he'd stepped in and set a course without having taken anybody else's opinion into account. No wonder his ship was feeling a little lost at sea. As a result, he'd been running with an ever-increasing risk of inefficiency and a lack of innovation and diversity of thought, while thinking he needed to be all things to all people.

Tom didn't actually want any of this, but the pressure he'd been under had created an accidental dictator. He was terrified of losing control, so only deferred to his two highest performers, Rachel and David. Yet he was intimidated by them and he never questioned them. I say this with great empathy because a lot of the mistakes Tom was making with his team, I'd made myself.

Group development

I like to introduce my clients, Tom included, to the Tuckman model, published in 1965.[10] It's an oldie, but a goodie. In fact, it's something that I had seen deployed numerous times throughout my early career, but back then, I never really understood what it meant or how it could be applied.

Tuckman's model looks at the stages of team development from the classic cycle of forming, storming, norming, performing. When people talk about a new team, generally they think about teams disbanding and a whole new group of people coming together. I'm a big believer that by adding or replacing just one person

---

10   B W Tuckman, 'Developmental Sequence in Small Groups', *Psychological Bulletin* (1965)

in a team, we create a whole new team. In a growing business, such as TBB, new staff are constantly arriving, so Tom was always dealing with new teams going through the stages of group development.

Forming

For a new team, we begin at the forming stage. Here people don't know each other and are polite as they test the waters. They aren't quite clear on their own and others' places in the team, or what their exact role will be. They look to the leader for guidance and wait to be told what they need to do. This is when the leader needs to be more hands on in making sure that people are clear on what their responsibilities will be. Once the team feels more comfortable, it can start to test the boundaries.

Storming

Now some team members act more independently in bringing ideas to the table and stating their areas of expertise. Here we can expect to see some conflict, and the metaphorical elbowing of each other as each team member finds their own space and place in the team.

Norming

As the team continues to develop, members begin to understand and respect each other more and the team becomes more than the sum of its parts. The members recognise that by working together, they will be stronger as a team, and the more cohesive the team is, the more it sets its procedures and direction of travel. Any concerns about differences among the team members are less important than how they will all work together.

Performing

In an ideal world, the team progresses to performing where people no longer even need to think about the team dynamics; they turn up and just get on and work. Instead of homing in on other people's differences, they focus on the work at hand. Quite simply, they get each other. They know all the boundaries, and where and how everyone fits.

That's what leaders want to see in terms of a team. But anyone leaving or joining this optimal team affects its overall dynamic, so the team needs to go through this whole process again to reform, otherwise any new person will always feel like the outsider trying to fit in, and possibly wary of stepping up to the plate.

How long it takes to move from forming to performing depends on the team, and what a leader is putting in place to support that team's development. When teams are dysfunctional or in conflict, there's often no underlying fundamental flaw; instead it's the result of stunted development during the storming stage.

A leader can help a team progress from forming through storming to norming and beyond by explicitly stating the scope of the team, the roles within it and what its goals are (I will discuss this more in the next chapter). The leader must also articulate clearly the team's values and its direction, such as what behaviours will be on display and what is acceptable.

Tom's team had been stuck at the storming stage for quite some time, and from what I'd observed, they were expending too much time and energy bashing off each other. They weren't cohesive and were forever pressing each other's buttons because Tom had been unable to set any clear direction or values on who they were and how they should operate.

Ultimately, I wanted to see Tom get to the point where he could stand back and empower his team so that its members could take the next step into the performing stage and simply get on with their jobs without his 'interference'. As soon as they know he recognises them as the subject-matter experts they are, they'll live and breathe the processes for themselves. The more Tom learns about leadership, the better equipped he'll be to understand how he can move his teams on and ensure any progress is smooth as possible. He is, after all, a technician at heart; he's logical and he likes certainty and detail.

Tom was suddenly quite passionate as he summed up his thinking. 'I thought this all was going to be really bloody hard. I thought I'd just be sitting here listening to you waffle on about some new-age blue-sky thinking, and that's just not me. But I've got to tell you, this is right up my street. It's logical. It's based on solid research.'

'Research borne out by experience.'

'That's why I'm sold!'

'Imagine what it'll feel like when your whole team is pulling together, with the same weight of passion behind each person. How much more will the business achieve?'

At this point, Ruth popped her head around the door. 'Sorry, Tom, but Mr Hennings-Moir from Marlow Beggs is here for his two o'clock with you.'

Tom glanced at his watch – it was five past two. We said our goodbyes and I told him I'd email him tomorrow with his homework, and with that, he was on his way to his next meeting. But not before making a final remark for the day.

'Next time, I'll keep the afternoon free. Book it in with Ruth and I'll tell her to clear everything else.'

TOM'S HOMEWORK

For his 'homework', I asked Tom to select a member of the team to coordinate this process. This person should not be a member of the senior leadership team. These were the instructions I then gave to him:

Ask team members to each answer these questions and submit their answers, by email, to the coordinator. Highlight to team members that they should answer these questions independently and not discuss their answers.

1. What is the real impact the work of your role/team has had on the end customer during the past year?

2. What are the skills, experience and/or capabilities required to achieve this value for our stakeholders or customers?

3. Name one positive team behaviour we need to display to achieve this value and to make best use of our skills, experience and capabilities captured in your previous responses?

For points 1 and 2, ask the coordinator to collate the responses on a spreadsheet, grouping similar responses together. Arrange a day where you can bring together fifteen people from across the organisation, representing all levels and teams (I pointed out that Tom should be one of the fifteen). Divide into three teams of five. The co-ordinator is to ask each team to use the information they'd gathered in the responses to points 1 and 2 to answer:

Vision:

- If you were to fast forward twenty years to find TBB has continued to thrive and is achieving everything we could ever have dreamed of, what would be the change it has made in the world?

Mission:

- Who is it that you're serving? Who are your customers? They might be outside the organisation, the end customer or your partners.
- What is the impact you're looking to bring or make?
- What is your approach to that?

Discuss the answers from the three groups and bring together the bare bones of a company vision and mission. These things take time, so this is just a start, but it is something that the team should continue to work on over the coming weeks and months.

For point three, perform a count and shortlist the top five or six behaviours submitted – circulate the shortlist and ask each team member to vote for their top three.

You have six weeks to complete these tasks. I will be back then to hear how you got on.

Tom did as he was asked. The team of fifteen, supported by the coordinator, gathered insights from the whole organisation. Distilling this information down was a challenge, but all involved were engaged and motivated. At last they were being heard.

Summary

Bringing all team members to one table isn't an automatic path to finding a solution. Yes, it's vital to consult different perspectives and different areas of expertise on a problem, but at the same time, we need to be mindful of team dynamics at play that can sometimes result in a team being less than the sum of its parts.

We always need to be on the lookout for groupthink – a situation, group or clique in which everyone gets on with each other famously with a great sense of bonhomie, but the desire to maintain harmony within the group is prioritised over critical thinking. Groupthink also excludes any team members who aren't part of the group, while the members themselves, in a bid to maintain harmony, can start to think as a collective rather than as individuals. This can lead to the Abilene paradox where no one in the group actually agrees to what the collective is saying, but they all go along with it as they think all the others do agree. And those excluded from the groupthink get fed up and ultimately lack trust in the company and its leaders as they can often see what is happening, but their voice isn't heard.

It's important for the leader to hold back their own opinion until others have spoken. This allows others present to offer their ideas. If a leader kicks off the meeting with their own opinions and then invites responses, it's highly unlikely that people will disagree with them and as a result may instigate or exacerbate groupthink or the Abilene paradox.

Finally in this chapter, we took a look at the Tuckman model, covering the four stages of team development: forming, storming, norming and performing. In this context, I don't necessarily mean a complete overhaul of a team; adding or replacing one person in an existing team effectively creates a new team ready for development. Ultimately, at the performing stage, the team members know all the boundaries, and where and how everyone fits in. That's what we as leaders want to see from our teams.

SIX

Clarify

15 November

I found myself back at TBB HQ in Cambridge. The winter was now well and truly here, the outside air was cool, and coats and scarves were part of my daily routine. As I parked my car, I was wondering how well Tom was responding to the first doses of the Vaccine.

We'd covered a lot of ground during our workshop and feedback discussions, which had addressed a number of leadership fundamentals. In the process, we'd created a basis for the framework ahead. I felt that Tom was, for the first time as CEO of TBB, giving himself the space he needed to create the right culture to allow him and his team to articulate their direction, purpose and vision, and consequently really know why their roles existed. With this pillar in place, it was only now that Tom and I would be able to move on to clarifying the scope and boundaries of his, the teams' and the overall business's roles and responsibilities. This was the time for Tom to understand why he was doing what he was doing, and what it actually was he was doing, by gaining the clarity he so desperately needed.

The power of niching

What was clear so far was that Tom had seen his business grow from a one-man band into an entity which employed fifty-five people as his initial client base had expanded rapidly over five years. As is common with many new ventures, he didn't find it easy to say no to clients and their increasingly diverse range of requests, and the more they asked Tom if he could take on new projects, the more he said yes. Slowly but surely, Tom had built up a whole suite of services. Some of these he now used for multiple clients with a set of established processes and systems, the remainder were on the periphery and were a little more reactive and un-systemised.

As a result, the business had grown based on client needs and in response to rapid ongoing developments within both the industry and TBB's competitors. From my perspective, there seemed to have been little proactive forward planning giving any proper consideration to whether new project X or new initiative Y was of any real value to the business.

Having been in Tom's shoes, I completely understood where he was coming from; I used to have clients approach me when I was a pharma consultant and ask if I could, for example, provide drug safety services for a particular type of clinical setting, even if I'd had no direct experience in that particular area. I'd always respond with, 'I've not done that before, but let me look into it to see what that entails, and I'll let you know whether or not I can do it.'

When we as leaders find ourselves in Tom's position, we must always be extra cautious and not simply rush in with 'Yes, we can' in response to a potential piece of work that sits on the edge of what we do. A knee-jerk response to taking on work to increase the revenue is the easiest of temptations to fall into. For the owner of any small business, especially in its early stages, it feels counterintuitive to turn work down. If the business is doing good work for a client that contributes to a large chunk of its revenue, and that client asks for some extra work that may, or may not, equate to significant additional revenue, the temptation is to accept the work anyway. It's not fear of losing the additional business that's at play here; it's the fear of losing the *total* business from that valuable client by turning down one particular job. If we can't offer an extra broad spectrum of services to the client, then a competitor might, and hey presto! The whole relationship is thwarted.

This had been Tom's main problem. He had recently taken on some additional consultancy work outside of TBB's direct subject-matter expertise for a long-standing client. Instead of agreeing to take it on, then performing under par (leading to some of his recent issues), Tom should have scoped the new project out in terms of capability, resource availability and potential profitability in advance. This was a costly error of judgement on Tom's part because to fulfil the client's needs, he had to spend extra money on training staff for that one-off project, which diverted people and resources away from his core business operations.

With core business offerings, there are established processes and degrees of automation giving capacity and scale that ultimately contribute towards profitability. It's not a problem particular to Tom; I often see a £50K turnover project that in fact only generates £1K in profit – once all the additional expenses to deliver it have been factored in – cause a leader far more interest and excitement than a core business project, which in spite of being worth only £10K in revenue, generates a far larger profit because it is supported by well-established processes.

Proactive planning and leadership clarity are key to understanding scope and generating profitability, otherwise services could be detrimental to the business, not only because they may cost more to deliver than they will bring in, but also because they run the risk of defining the business as a jack of all trades, master of none. With this in mind, today, I decided to discuss with Tom the power of niching and how it is vital in terms of selling TBB's services and staking its place in the market. It also prevents personnel taking on projects which don't suit them or are beyond their competencies.

'I guess I've always been scared of saying no to a client,' Tom said, 'but on this last occasion, we probably should have turned the job down. But Stacey's one of my biggest clients; she's been on our books since we began, and I didn't want to put that relationship in jeopardy.'

'Except now you're trying to fire-fight a major compliance issue because TBB wasn't the right fit in the first place.'

'Yes. It's been a bit of nightmare, to be honest, and I think it's only because we and Stacey go back a long way that we've got through by the skin of our teeth.'

'It still kept you awake at night, though, didn't it? All that angst for something that TBB's not even known for doing.'

'As I said, I was scared what Stacey and her business would do if we turned it down.'

'I understand. It's natural for any business that's looking to grow, like yours is. But sometimes, we can't allow ourselves to make that type of decision based on the fear of saying no to a client. If you don't believe that something's right for you at the time, it's important to be transparent, and believe me, your clients will respect you more if you say, "You know what? We're not the right company to do that for you" than if you take it on and then mess it up.

'In fact, it actually happened to me just the other day. I had to say no to a potential training project because I felt I wasn't the right person to deliver what the client needed. What I did do was help them find the right company to solve their problem.'

'How did that turn out for you?'

'The client respected me so much for doing that, they offered me another project that was well within my scope.'

Transparency wins

'Not wanting to say no to clients – the curse of the SME, eh?'

'Not at all, I see this happening in big business all the time as well. The principles are the same. Someone who heads up a team or department gets told to deliver a project on the periphery of their team's experience or expertise. Instead of being scared they might be demoted or side-lined by their leaders in the future if they say no, what they could do is either tell them, 'Yes, of course we'll take it on because it's a regulatory requirement, but please know this is something I need to upskill, or I need to look at my resources before confirming I can deliver this', or be brave and share their thoughts if they feel that another team may be better suited.

'It's about being transparent and having the discussion, even at the risk of it not going your way, not being a "yes man". It's about having integrity and managing expectations, not simply trying to please people.'

I could guess what Tom was thinking. Not only had taking on this new work cost the business money, it had almost cost it its reputation. If it weren't for the fact that Tom was one of life's genuine people who was personally well-liked and respected within his industry, things might have been different.

He stirred his coffee for the umpteenth time, deep in thought. Then out of the blue, he said, 'Even just by having this conversation, I must admit, I feel a little bit silly that we're doing all of this. You know, putting in a huge amount of effort, a huge amount of churn. And you're right, that's what keeps me up at night, and all those bloody additional processes that...'

He suddenly looked uncomfortable.

'That, what?' I pressed him.

'That I don't really understand.'

This felt like a huge moment for Tom and I let him think it through a little longer. I didn't want to put words into his mouth. A couple of minutes later, he continued.

'I feel like, as the so-called "leader" in this business, I'm meant to be the one that knows more than anyone about these processes. Truth is, I don't. I'm just as much in the dark as the rest of them. And that makes me feel a bit nervous. I don't understand the mechanics for these processes because they're not things I've personally ever worked on.'

'But that's great, Tom, that gives us a really good insight into what we need to work on next.'

'It does?'

'Absolutely. First off, ask yourself, in the light of what we've just talked about, "What is TBB?" Do you remember when I first asked you that same question, when I was doing my background preparation for the Strategy day? And I asked you, "Who is TBB? What services do you provide to the industry?" What was your response?'

Tom smiled, recollecting that moment. 'I remember it well. I said, "Where should I start?" I told you the business kicked off with its core offerings, but now we did a bit of this, a bit of that – basically whatever the clients need.'

'Exactly. I don't think you really thought that was a problem then, and that was only a few weeks ago.'

'Hard to believe, really, considering where it all started five years ago.'

How to start clarifying scope

'The easiest way to start clarifying your scope is to consider what you would say is the one thing TBB is really good at. What is it that you would be best known for? Think of all of the work you've been doing these past weeks with the team around the impact you have on your end customer.'

'Easy. Our four core processes. That's what the industry wants, and that's what we give it in spades. Nobody does these better than us – not a business our size, at least. You know, it's strange, but I noticed that when the team spoke about the core processes, there was a palpable sense of pride – excitement, even.'

'Good. And what makes you good? What makes you the best?'

'Everyone knows what they're doing so well, they can do it blindfolded.'

'I'm really pleased you said that, Tom, because what I've noticed is that with those four core processes, you seem more able and happy to delegate responsibility. You don't feel the need to be at the centre of them the whole time.'

'I don't need to. I devised those processes, everyone's been trained. I only get involved when there is an issue such as someone not following the process.'

'OK, so what are you not so great at?'

'What do you mean?'

'If things are great in that area, how come you're kept awake at night?'

'I see. There're lots of things I'm not great at. Is that what you mean?'

'What about your current compliance issues? Your audit reports? Any customer complaints? What are they?'

'Ah, now I get you. That's easy. It's those few processes we only do for a couple of clients. They're the ones we just can't get a handle on, such as how much resource we need to devote to them. At the moment, we've got four people who between them do up to twelve different processes each, but we're finding it really difficult to keep all this documented. We can't invest any more time in writing them up, simply because they don't bring us in a huge amount of money.'

'Whereas the four core processes do?'

'Exactly.'

'So why do these extra projects?'

'OK, I see your point, but as I said, when clients like Stacey ask us to do a bit extra, we just fall into taking it all on. We don't want to say no for all the reasons we've talked about. Then we divvy the jobs out to the same people every time.'

'Are the core processes you provide profitable?'

'Of course! The margins are excellent. I can reel them off if you like.'

'No need. What about the additional peripheral activities you've taken on, how profitable are they?'

'I don't know. I'd have to look them up. Not very, I imagine. In fact, I know that quite a few are loss making.'

'How does that make you feel?'

'Anxious, full of doubt, asking myself, "Why did we bother? Do we need them?" I don't have the answers.'

'I look at it like this: it's fine to have new processes in your business that you haven't worked on before.

Your business is expanding, but you're no longer the lead technician; you're the CEO leading the business. That's where your attention needs to be focused: in understanding what your value proposition is. What is it that you bring to the industry? What is it that you're phenomenal at in serving your customers? To get there, always go back to your vision, so that when you do bring on new processes, you don't leave them on the periphery. Instead, you make them part of your core offering. After all, if you are going to take the time and effort to set them up and implement them for one client, you may as well do so for many. As you do, you'll see the confidence, efficiency and profitability increase.'

Currently, Tom's core processes were like four plates on a table. He knew where they were, he knew everything about them. Sometimes the table might need to move and be reset, but he had complete confidence in them.

There were also a dozen peripheral processes which were like spinning plates. Tom felt that if he didn't keep spinning them, they'd fall to the ground and smash. And at some point, make no mistake, they would fall, because the technicians working on them didn't fully understand the processes either. The problem was compounded because for those technicians, these jobs weren't full-time commitments; they were the 'odd-jobs' for a handful of clients, and the technicians didn't have the time to invest in getting to know them better.

That was what was keeping Tom awake at night. His technicians couldn't be expected to be dedicated subject-matter experts, so he was having to spin all of the plates himself. He was overstretched and continually having to play catch up, having over-committed to taking on misaligned projects without having the right resources or skills to execute them.

In reality, he could have briefed one of his managers, Linda, with the project spec for his client, Stacey, and had an up-front scoping discussion. Instead, Linda hadn't been part of that discussion. Tom went ahead and wrote up the proposal without any real inkling of how the business was going to pull it off, and when it was all signed and sealed, that was when it landed on Linda's desk, much to her horror and dismay. For her, it was another process to manage when she still wasn't fully up to speed on the others Tom had thrown over the fence to her already.

This approach bred a negative cycle of inevitable defeatism. Linda was trying to run uphill backwards on a daily basis, worried out of her skin that she'd screw up at some point, and when she did, Chris would be down on her like a ton of bricks. All because Tom found it hard to ask how a project could be best handled and by whom, if at all.

In the great scheme of things, that should have been an easy discussion to have. Then, working as a team, everyone would have understood that this could potentially be a difficult project. With this knowledge from the outset, they could have navigated it together, which would have allowed them (Tom included) to better understand why they were taking on the new project in the first place. Tom could now see that trust must coexist between a leader and their teams as this would help motivate people to take ownership and seek solutions.

Scope paralysis

Where lines are blurred on who does or owns what, something I term 'scope paralysis' ensues. Nobody knows who's responsible for anything. In Tom's case, that had been the root cause of the company's compliance issues and the twelve processes causing the issues.

Tom had already over-extended himself. This was then compounded by scope paralysis as Linda and her colleagues had no idea who was responsible for fixing the holes in the processes, given that Tom was traditionally the one who wrote them up. But on this occasion, he'd lobbed them over the wall to Linda because he himself was unsure about what needed to be done. In the end, everyone lost sight of what they were actually good at, and Tom's belief that his team could turn the processes around into something meaningful was misguided. For the team, it felt as if they were doing him a favour.

No matter how great our culture is, if our team members believe they're constantly doing us as the leader a favour, they'll disown responsibility for doing a job well because they feel under-skilled, or under-resourced.

This can, in turn, lead to massive stress. That was precisely how Linda and her colleagues were feeling about the extra jobs Tom had agreed to take on without proper commercial consideration.

SCOPE PARALYSIS EXPLAINED

What exactly is scope paralysis? Let me explain what I mean with a little analogy.

Imagine I'm in my workplace and I'm heading into the office kitchen. As I open the kitchen door, my colleague Jim is on his way out.

I say to him politely, 'After you, Jim.'

'No, Rebecca, after you,' he replies. And now we're stuck in a merry little polite dance, nobody knowing who is to go through the door first.

This is what happens if you're a leader who is not clear on the scope, remit and boundaries of your teams' responsibilities. If you aren't clear, how on earth can your team members be clear? What ends up happening is instead of your team members coming in and getting on with their work, as they get closer to the edge of the boundaries of their responsibilities, they get stuck in a no man's land where they're not sure on whether something is their job or their colleague's or the interfacing team's job. They don't want to step on anybody's toes, so either they slow down, which causes inefficiency, or worse still, they retract, stepping back, leaving a gaping chasm between them and the interfacing team. This may be one of the other teams in their department or another department, it may be business partners, or it may be the client's team. Unchecked and unresolved, this can lead to significant non-compliance issues.

If you want to ensure against such inefficiency and non-compliance, you need to be 100% clear. Clarify the scope for each and every one of your team members. Clarify who owns, does and is involved in each task.

At TBB, I decided to run a simple but clearly defined activity with Linda and her colleagues, and I invited Tom to sit and observe. I gave each person a large pile of oversized Post-it notes and asked them to write every task and break out every activity that they did in respect of the company's processes. Using the four walls of the room, on one wall I created a label 'We do', explaining that this wall was for activities and tasks that were aligned to the company's developing vision and purpose. Another wall was 'We don't do' for tasks and activities that were not aligned with the purpose. The third wall was dedicated to 'Not sure' for activities that needed further discussion to clarify whether they were in scope, and the fourth wall was for what they weren't yet doing, but really felt that they should be doing.

Two days and 285 Post-it notes later, a picture began to emerge. Each person presented back to the group what each task or activity was and why they'd placed them where they had. It certainly generated some heated debate and disagreements, but it also began to find a natural commonality of themes and eye-opening revelations as to where activities overlapped between colleagues. It also gave each member of the team a clear view on what they and each of their colleagues were actually doing in their role.

At the end of the two days, I invited Tom to plot the activities based on each process and create a bar chart which clearly showed the percentage that were aligned to the purpose and vision of the business, or not. The exercise revealed a staggering 40% of effort in some areas was being spent on processes and projects mis-aligned to the organisation's direction and purpose.

TBB'S SCOPING PLOT

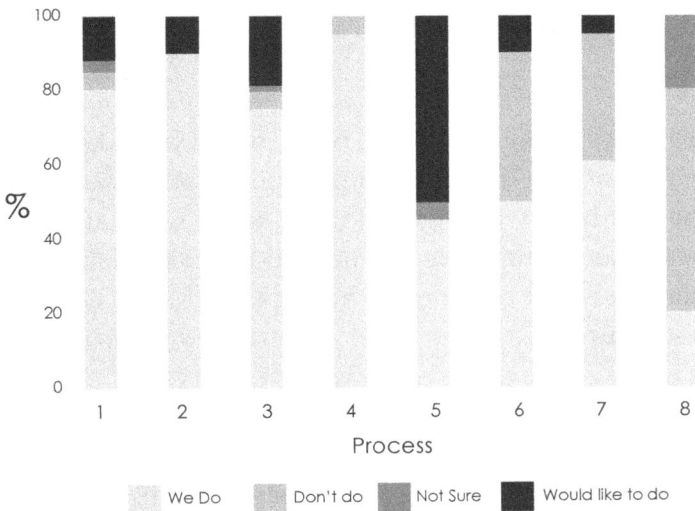

As you can see in this plot showing eight of the company's processes, in processes 1 to 4 (TBB's core processes), the vast majority of tasks are in the 'we do', or aligned to purpose, category, with a small proportion of activites which the team would like to do, but do not currently do.

In process 6, 7 and, in particular, 8, there is a significant proportion of tasks being performed that are misaligned to purpose, activities that are not adding value to the business.

However, in process 5, another one of the twelve 'periphery processes', most of the activities that the team are currently performing are aligned to purpose, and there is a significant proportion of activities not yet being performed that the team feel are aligned to the vision and would drive the business forward.

By releasing resource from misaligned activites, Tom could free up time and expertise to explore the tasks that his teams would like to do.

To Tom's astonishment, he realised that he did in fact have enough resources to perform a lot of the tasks he had been wanting to do, but never felt that there was enough time. He just needed to cut the activities that were not serving the business and its vision for the future.

I asked him if he'd be prepared to repeat this scoping exercise himself with a broader cross-section of his employees, which he instantly agreed to. He was keen to enable all team members to have the opportunity to clearly understand and articulate the scope of their own roles and responsibilities. As soon as they could fully own the tasks within their processes, they would execute those tasks with greater conviction, leading to a significant improvement in team morale and unity.

A week later

22 November

Returning to TBB the following week to check in with Tom's progress, I was surprised firstly to find that Tom was already waiting for me in the conference room (I double checked my watch to make sure it wasn't me who was running late – I wasn't). Secondly, Tom immediately informed me that he'd gone back to a major client with the news that TBB would no longer continue to service a peripheral project once the current contract came to term on the basis his company couldn't provide the best value.

But he was saving the biggest win to last. 'Guess what? They said they are sick of working with people who are yes men and they're really thrilled that I've been so transparent, and as a result they've offered us a fantastic contract based on three of our periphery processes and . . . '

He could hardly contain his excitement as he continued.

'Because we've gone through the scoping exercise, we know this extra work is perfectly aligned to our overall vision and mission. Plus, we already know exactly who can act as project leads without causing any extra stress or conflict. It's a profitable additional contract for us, not like the arrangement we had in place before. I've asked David and Linda to look into this, because I think we can build on it. It makes complete sense to push these three extra processes to other clients with the same precision as we do on our four core processes, so we now have seven core processes!'

'Does that mean you can turn those extra three processes into proactive sales funnels?'

'Yes, that's exactly what it means.'

'Great! You can start to scale after all and control it instead of taking on projects that were eating into your resources.'

'I know, mad isn't it? The answer was right under our noses all the time.'

'What's the biggest takeaway from all of this, Tom?'

'Easy. Now we've – I've – gone through this scoping exercise and understood what that means for each and every one of us in the team, I know what our capabilities are and how they align to our vision and mission. I have complete clarity. I know who TBB is. And so does everyone else who walks through those doors every morning.'

Reflections

From my perspective as a leadership strategist, it's always important to understand how overwhelming holistic change can initially be not just for people such as Tom who are really passionate about their organisation, but also for those who head up teams in large companies. When Tom realised my function wasn't to come into his business to order him to change, I noticed him visibly relaxing. Instead, he realised it was about him understanding that he already had the tools at his fingertips and just needed to explore the practical steps to unlock his leadership potential.

I could see that he was beginning to piece his own puzzle together and that the Vaccine was taking hold; already he'd worked on his mission and vision, and he was now clarifying with his team what the business is, and what they do and do not do. Leadership was gradually seeming a little less lonely because the team members were with him rather than against him, and they were no longer 100% dependent on him. As a result, he was feeling more understood.

Now that his team was a cohesive unit working off the same page, Tom could actively find more time to dedicate to developing his leadership skills through our workshops and sessions. The big turning point for him was that in working on his leadership skills, he harnessed the ability to make scaling the business more of a reality. With scale would come more responsibility, but now it wasn't an issue that would keep him awake at night because he relished those opportunities. It helped massively that he was learning to delegate many of the day-to-day operations as and when required with a confidence he'd never experienced before.

Tom's journey reminds me of how it felt when I was in a similar position – that moment when I reached the one-year anniversary in my role and for the first time since I'd found myself leading, I did something for the second time. I still had the same amount of responsibility, the same financial and personal pressures, but it felt different. It felt like a positive pressure, rather than a drowning pressure.

I knew that for Tom, he was beginning to feel like a leader and not like someone who'd accidentally ended up in the wrong seat. As CEO, he was seeing that the majority of his time shouldn't be spent on revenue generating activities. The best way he could contribute to generating revenue was by leading the company.

SCOPING WORKS FOR ANY SIZE OF BUSINESS

On the face of it, some aspects of Tom's story may only seem applicable to service-based small businesses, but please do not be fooled. In actual fact, I developed the scoping exercise described in this chapter for a global team I led in a top ten pharma company. We used the exercise to really understand what our team stood for;

what we did and where the areas were that were causing stress, because we felt we were left holding a baby that was not ours to hold; what we needed to stop doing and what we needed to start doing. Simply by identifying areas that we felt were either already or better served by other teams, we were able to free up resources, which allowed us to take on activities key to our core purpose that we had not previously had the time to work on.

It's incredible the response you get from stakeholders and partners when you share with them your thoughts on the activity you've been doing and how you feel it's important to provide the best service, be that to clients or to internal customers. Sharing the detail of the outputs demonstrates an intent to truly ensure that all bases are covered by those who are best placed as opposed to simply passing the buck. Try it – you'll likely be surprised.

SCOPING WALLS

It may well be beneficial for you and your teams to have a go at the scoping exercise that proved so valuable to Tom, Linda and everyone at TBB, so here it is for you to follow.

Set aside a day or two to gather as a team for this activity. Establish an environment to ensure you all focus on the task at hand, eg encourage a phone/laptop-off rule and make sure all team members are involved in the activity.

Ask each team member to list on large Post-it notes all of the tasks they perform and any activities they do not currently perform but believe that they should perform to fulfil their role. Determine in advance how detailed you plan to be as a team. I suggest keeping detail to activity level rather than overall process level as some processes may be cross-functional or be shared between more than one team.

Label each of the four walls in the room/four flip charts:

- 'We do' – tasks the teams are currently performing that they consider to be clearly within their scope
- 'We don't do' – tasks the teams are currently performing that they don't consider to be within their scope
- 'Not sure' – tasks the teams are currently performing, but they are not clear if they are within their scope
- 'Would like to do' – tasks the teams are not currently performing that are clearly within their scope

Invite team members one at a time to present their listed activities and place them on the wall/chart that they and the group feel best fits that task/activity. Discuss until the group are agreed on the contents of each of the four walls.

Capture the listed activities on a spreadsheet under each business process noting which category each activity is considered to be in, eg "we do". Plot the number of activities in each category on a clustered bar chart grouped by process to identify the process that requires the most attention in terms of unclear or ill-defined scope. Review the activities listed in each category. Clarify through discussion whether those in the 'not sure' category are in or out of the team's scope. Where activities are considered out of scope, take steps to stop, delegate or transfer these activities, e.g. to another team. By transferring, delegating or ceasing activities that are out of scope, you will allow more focus and time to be spent on the activities and tasks that are key to fulfilling the role of your team or in meeting your ideal client's needs.

Working through this exercise as a team ensures inclusion and subsequent commitment, as well as raising awareness as to the scope and activities of all team members.

Summary

Leadership Vaccine Tenet Three:

CLARIFY the scope and boundaries of your team responsibilities and activities.

Ensure seamless links with interfacing organisations and teams, thereby removing gaps and/or duplication in cross-functional projects and processes.

In this chapter, having got the first pillar, Culture, in place, we start to look at the second – the scope of Tom's role, and that of his teams and the business as a whole. I fully understand, having been in the same position myself, how difficult it is for a new leader to say no to any client request. As a result, Tom has built up a suite of services without much appreciation of whether each one actually brings any value to the business.

When any leader finds themselves in the position of always saying yes to clients, they need to make sure they scope out the resources and capabilities required to deliver that extra service or product, and the potential profitability it offers. With core business offerings, there are established processes and degrees of automation giving capacity and scale that ultimately contribute towards profitability. Proactive planning and leadership clarity are key to understanding scope and generating profitability. Taking on business not suited to the company's vision, mission and values could not only cost it money, but also its reputation if it starts to become known as a jack of all trades, master of none.

Having discussed the concepts of niching and being transparent about whether or not the business is the right fit for each project that comes along, Tom and I then move into the realm of clarifying scope. The scope of the business is essentially its core offerings, the things the founder would want the business to be remembered for. If a business is considering taking on a project outside of this core, all stakeholders need to be involved in the preliminary discussions so they can go into it (or not) fully informed on what it will entail. Without this clarity, leaders, teams and even whole businesses become victims of scope paralysis, where nobody knows who owns what role. No matter how great a culture is, if team members believe they're constantly doing the leader a favour, they'll disown responsibility for doing a job well.

Tom's major takeaway from the concepts we've covered in this chapter is that clarity is king when it comes to scope, with the result that a major client is so delighted with TBB's honesty and transparency, they offer a major contract for three of the peripheral processes that can now become core to the business. And best of all, every single person on his team, himself included, now knows exactly what TBB stands for.

SEVEN

Create

So often when people talk about leadership development, they believe that the most important (possibly even the only) elements are creating the right culture and facilitating staff development. Of course, these play an integral part, but they are only two of the five pillars that underpin the fabric of the Leadership Vaccine:

1. Culture

2. Scope

3. Structure

4. Staff development

5. Process

Scoping, as we have seen in the previous chapter, process and structure are equally vital. If these areas are ignored or set incorrectly, then no matter how much you write beautifully inspiring vision and mission statements, or how much time you spend in developing yourself and your team, the resilience of your business is diminished and you fail to empower or engage the people you work with.

It's a familiar story

I chose to reflect Tom's journey in discovering his leadership skills in this book because so many of his 'aha' moments along the way mirrored my own within the big pharma sector. He and I both found ourselves occupying the accidental leader's chair. As a scientist working in the pharmaceutical industry, and as a highly qualified subject-matter expert, I was subsequently unprepared for the juggernaut of responsibility that hit me at high speed when I stepped out on to the career highway. By the time I'd reached the destination of being the person whole teams and departments looked to for direction, it was overwhelming. There simply was no time, or space, to slip under the barrier, find a quiet layby, pour myself a mug of tea from a Thermos flask and reflect, 'How the hell did I get here?'

In Tom's case, he was the CEO of his own business that had grown at a pace that outran him. Like me, he was a subject-matter expert who was totally unprepared for the role of leader that he was trying his best to hold down. There was nobody for him to report in to; the buck always stopped with him. His only way of coping with leadership was to try and control everything, and without any guidance or framework, such as the pillars that I was introducing to him, he was at risk of drowning under the weight of responsibility. Since we'd worked our way through the intricacies of culture and scope, though, he was not only floating to the surface, he was getting ready to swim the English Channel.

Culture had shown him that vision, mission and values shared among the whole team, even with the likes of his polar opposite, big-picture thinking Chris, would create common ground on which they all could develop and build. Tom was now aware that beyond his clique of David and Rachel, there were other voices and opinions equally as valid and impactful on team performance and deliverability.

In gaining clarity on scope, where once the business had been in danger of retracting, the teams now worked together and identified what worked for them, what didn't and where they could transfer responsibilities and execution to team members who could manage different processes. As a result, the business was in a better position to scale, but more significantly, people knew with confidence what TBB stood for and what it did. They understood their purpose within that and were in alignment with Tom, and he was confident that he no longer needed to run the operation on a command

and control basis. His team members had become more motivated with the room to spread their own wings and fly. They could actually make important decisions without fear of screwing up if they didn't run them by Tom beforehand.

My next meeting with Tom

17 December

When I next met with Tom, as he showed me into his office, he asked, 'So, we're all done now. We've got this leadership lark all wrapped up.' I could tell he was joking because at the beginning of our work together, he'd never have been relaxed enough to say something so blatantly flippant. Not to me, at least.

'If only if were that simple, Tom.' I smiled back at him. 'But we're not that far off and I can see how much difference The Leadership Vaccine process is making already.'

And it was. The office vibe was palpably different to the one that I'd first walked into on that hot summer's day only a few months ago. Now, I could sense a real buzz as people seemed actively engaged with their clients on their headsets, and with each other. Tom greeted people by name as we walked towards his office, and he even stopped momentarily to ask Sophie about her cat. When Ruth spotted me across the floor and brought me in a coffee just the way I like it soon after, her eyes seemed to sparkle more and her brow no longer arched its way upwards. Now, it was time to put the seal on all our positive developments thus far and allow the Vaccine to work its magic on the structure of TBB.

In terms of organisational structure, be that horizontal or vertical, when it comes to the organisation chart, the key aim is to ensure that it demonstrates how each and every person fits into the business. The organisation structure should be designed in such a way that employees clearly know who they can talk to about things they can only talk to a line manager about, for example taking time off or dealing with a personal problem.

When I talk about creating the right structure, it's not only in terms of the organisation chart itself, it's also in terms of mindset. What I specifically mean by that is regardless of the organisation chart, we need to define where responsibilities are delegated and where people are empowered to work within that structure without any unnecessary deference to hierarchy. When I explained this to Tom, he looked interestedly puzzled. Yes, he was learning fast about delegation, but residual habits die hard, even if they were now only thoughts and not reactions.

I explained further. 'OK, Tom, if you're working on a particular project, you don't always need to be the subject-matter expert.'

If I'd said that to Tom on day one, he might well have burst a blood vessel, given his proclivity for control.

'It's alright, I'm OK,' he said, wiping a hand across his brow in mock relief.

'Like I knew you would be,' I continued, 'but let me clarify what I mean. Last time, we spoke about your team of four who were working on the twelve peripheral processes. I suggested you should tell Linda that from now on, she would own this, but that she could ask for your help as and when she needed it. In essence, you were going to suggest she run with it, doing the research and getting up to speed with the legislation. You would only be there as a sounding board.'

'Yep, and that seems to be working just fine, so far.'

'Good. So, let's look at how that's represented visually.'

I explained to Tom that up until now, the way he'd run the business saw him as the subject-matter expert. He'd been the one person who signed off every decision and every project, and that had been the cause of the bottlenecks.

In reality, what he should have been considering was that the majority of the subject-matter expertise actually needed to reside in the more junior levels. I could still see Tom flinching a little when I suggested this. What I wanted to persuade him to do was completely change that thought process and behaviour so that as and when an employee asked his opinion, Tom only needed to know enough about their systems and the legislation to be available for consultation. Tom didn't need to be the person with all the answers, but what he could be was a guiding hand, checking that all perspectives had been covered. Asking the right questions to elicit the right answer rather than giving out answers without chance for colleague input.

'We're moving TBB away from its traditional hierarchical structure,' I said.

'Interesting,' he replied. 'I was having dinner with an old friend of mine. He runs his own business, similar size to us, and I was telling him about the work you and I have been doing together. He nearly had a blue fit when I mentioned that I was learning to delegate more because he thinks the old way is the best way. Plus, he said he'd be worried about what would happen legally if something went wrong. Who'd be responsible if he'd delegated out and it ended up in court?'

'Yes, I'm familiar with that train of thought.'

Tom, as CEO, would still be ultimately accountable for the business legally, but that didn't mean he needed to be responsible for actually doing everything.

The RACI matrix

I explained to Tom that when people hold highly accountable roles, a responsible, accountable, consult, inform (RACI) matrix can help to ensure everything is in place, confirmed and clear to all, while also alleviating nerves, especially when it's hard to let go and delegate. The RACI matrix is an incredibly practical tool that identifies who's responsible for what.

'It means, Tom, in practical terms, you as the accountable person can immediately see who you can rely on to take the lead on a project. And it's so important for your team to know that, too. It's you telling Rachel, for example, that she's responsible for a designated task, and that David will be consulted or simply informed in this area, whichever is appropriate. If your teams aren't clear on who's responsible, accountable, consulted or informed, somebody who's actually responsible may think they're just being informed, and they'll end up not doing what they need to do.'

Tom nodded. It was another 'aha' moment.

'The RACI matrix is you proactively having a discussion with your team and being 100% clear on what you need from each member. If someone then pipes up and says they'd rather be consulted than simply informed, you can discuss that there and then. Because, in all likelihood, they do know best.

'Before, you never had these discussions; you simply lobbed things over fences and hoped they landed in the right place. Except nobody really knew what to do with the task once they'd picked it up, or who was responsible for it. You mistook that for delegation. That's why you continually created bottlenecks and a team of unhappy people around you. They were waiting to be told what to do by you – not exactly an inspiring way to spend a day at the office. In the end, you'd have to pick it up again yourself and sort out any problems – ones which you'd compounded in the first place. You were working way below your pay grade. By that, I mean you were costing the business money by taking on tasks that someone with a much lower salary could do.'

'I'd never thought of it like that before. I guess because it's my company, I don't think of costing my time out like that.'

'There's no such thing as free time at work, is there? What you could be doing more of with your high-cost time is training up people who could do a really great job for a lot less than what it's been costing you to do the same thing. The payoff is that you help people to expand and feel empowered. It goes back to Frederick Herzberg's hygiene and motivating factors. Enabling people to achieve and feel their own personal growth will motivate them a lot more than money ever will. Ultimately, it's these factors that will help you realise your ambition to scale the business, too.'

THE RACI MATRIX – A BIT OF BACKGROUND

The term RACI has been around for a long time. When writing this book, I was keen to explain its historical origins, but I have found this rather difficult. Some cite NASA as having come up with the concept, others say that it originated from goal directed project management methodology, which first arose in the early 1970s. Andersen, Grude and Haug's book *Goal Directed Project Management* was first published in 1984.[11]

The term itself comes from the first letter of each part of the method – responsible, accountable, consult and inform. You simply plot out the responsibilities of each party against R, A, C, I.

For example:

	R	A	C	I
Process X	John	Sue	Peter, Sandeep	Claire

In this example, Sue is accountable for the process. There should only be one name in the accountable box as this person is, in the vast majority of cases, the one who signs off the work, has the final decision and ultimately owns the process.

Here, Sue has delegated the doing of the work to John, who is responsible for ensuring it is completed to the appropriate standard. In doing this work, John must

---

11   E S Andersen, K V Grude, T Haug, *Goal Directed Project Management: Effective techniques and strategies* (Kogan Page, 2009, fourth edn)

consult with and may seek advice from Peter and Sandeep, all the time keeping Claire informed as to the progress of the process and any issues that might arise. Claire will not be consulted on decisions before they are made but must be informed of all decisions.

This simple tool allows for controlled delegation, clarification of role definitions and oversight of what each member of the team is bringing to the project. It's all planned and outlined so that the leader can allow the team to get on with their work without needing hands-on control at all times.

Up until now, Tom had been so focused on trying to get back on track so that he could scale, this was the first time he'd started to see for himself that the practical steps we'd worked through together could also make a personal difference to the way he felt about his job. Like so many CEOs and managing directors I meet who run the operational aspects of their own businesses, Tom had never regarded himself as an employee of his business, but that's exactly what he was.

As an employee, Tom had certain rights and freedoms. He shouldn't have been working all hours, tied to his bleeping phone. Like anybody else, he was entitled to a good night's sleep.

Like Tom, so many company founders feel that they have to perform their leader's role by being wholly consumed by the business, because it's *their* business.

The irony is that while they might think they're the ones doing this to themselves, if they're anything like Tom, who has built a highly successful business, then the business has become a ravenous creature that's biting the owner's hand. Anything that Tom did to change the business in positive ways, the business in return would behave better towards him.

To that end, the business was rapidly undergoing transformation, led by Tom's example. All the shifts and pivots he had put into practice, both personally and professionally, were having an impact on not only him, but also the people around him, and the business as a whole. His position had changed from 'this is me trying to scale' to 'this is us scaling'.

I know myself how it feels to build something with a team rather than do it from a high perch of leadership loneliness. It's hugely empowering as it dilutes much of the top-tier pressure and worry. For Tom, this was a massive relief. He knew he was ultimately responsible for safeguarding the salaries and building the careers of his team. From day one, he'd always been conscious of wanting to do the right thing by each and every one of them. He just didn't know how.

Building in resilience

An analogy of the importance of distributing control to build in resilience that really resonates with me, for obvious reasons, is shared in Jurgen Appelo's book *Managing for Happiness*.[12] He reminds us that the human body doesn't have just one master T cell in our immune system, it has millions. As a result, when one such cell is attacked, the whole system doesn't crumble. We see this throughout our bodies where distribution of control and built-in redundancy makes us resilient.

Tom was really enjoying this metaphorical conversation not only because it appealed to his scientific brain, but also because he completely related it to his business. If he were to neglect to implement any of the changes we'd worked on thus far, and he was 'attacked' as the holder of all the knowledge with all the key client relationships mediated through him, there would be no coming back for the business. Now that he was delegating and empowering his team members more, Tom could afford to be sick or take time off. He might even take a holiday!

For Tom and his position within TBB, this was a truly radical change – and one that he knew was needed. Much to his embarrassment, for too long, he'd appeared to the outside world like a dictator. That couldn't be further from the truth. In actuality, he was a forty-one-year-old scared little kid like Tom Hanks in *Big* who didn't know how to fill his size-11 leadership shoes.

---

12 J Appelo, *Managing for Happiness: Games, tools, and practices to motivate any team* (John Wiley & Sons, 2016)

We scrutinised the range of skills he was currently employing across his whole team, and I pointed out that Tom should look to see which people were the right fit, or had the potential to be the right fit, in terms of skills and experience for a particular process and where he could match his administrators to those processes.

In my experience in the pharmaceutical industry, administrators are absolutely invaluable to partner with when you're managing and running processes. They bring with them superior organisational skills and are unbiased in respect of technical knowledge. As a result, they often see gaps or issues in processes long before they become compliance issues. Partnering an administrator with a consultant can lead to absolute magic.

If Tom were to extend the principles of distributed control and shoring up resilience in his company, it would not only automatically improve his bottom line, because the profitability would change based on decreased costs per service, it would also lay the foundations for much needed succession planning and allow TBB to reap the benefits of all the diverse talent and experience it had within its staff pool.

'Tom, what would happen to the business if you were hit by a bus this afternoon? And didn't make it?'

It was a hard-hitting question to throw at Tom, especially following the great progress we were making in delving deep into the corners of the business that he'd never been able to explore for himself – or dared to, if he was being truly honest. His brow furrowed. Deep in thought, he stood up and walked towards the glass partition that separated his office from the world he had created beyond on the fourth floor. I didn't want to interrupt his thought processes so waited for his response to form.

As he sat down behind his desk again, he raised his right hand to his face and tapped his cheek a few times. Eventually, he replied.

'That's a good question. And a really hard one to answer. I know where you're going with this. In all honesty, I don't know. I don't have an answer that I can say, with hand on heart, would be the truth.'

'What are you thinking? Off the top of your head?'

'A couple of months back, before you started working with us, my wife was telling me about a chap at her firm, Roger. Late fifties, really great at what he did. Reliably old school, if you know what I mean. Always in the office, always hustling, hands-on kind of guy, brilliant at figures, just never seemed to go home. He was like a permanent fixture, according to my wife.

'One morning, he didn't show up. Wasn't like him. Couple of hours later, the office got the call. Heart attack. Gone. Dead. Just like that. No warning. Really hit his colleagues for six.'

'What about your wife?'

'She told me that would be me one day.'

'Why did she say that?'

'Oh, come on, she had a point. I've practically been living here these last few years. Not taken a day off, not even a sick day, in spite of having felt pretty ropey at times. I told her she didn't understand. It was different for her, she was "just" an employee – that didn't go down well, by the way – whereas this is my business and I have to be here. I've got responsibilities, blah, blah, blah. Crazy, eh? My own business and it won't let me go.'

'Oh, I completely get it. Sometimes when we say, "I need to be here", we really believe what we're saying.'

'Really? I think I'm beginning to see things a little bit differently these days. And it has nothing to do with Roger, that's the sad thing about it. The good thing is, these last couple of weeks, I've spent more time at home. We've even been out on a "date night" together. I'm seeing things from my wife's point of view. I only wish I'd done it a long time ago.'

'Listen, I know loads of senior people who are not there for their partners, their kids, their friends. And there's nothing worse than when someone turns to you and says, "There's more to life than your job." The truth is, when you're in the trenches, it's difficult to stick your head up and take a good look around. I'm so pleased you can see the light at the end of the tunnel. Being a leader isn't just about being at work. Sometimes you have to let go. It's knowing how, that's the trick.

'We all need to adapt as the world becomes ever more complex. With complex challenges, you need complex approaches, and you have this complexity among your staff. If you walk through the office and people are just doing what they're told, the business will be missing a massive amount of knowledge, expertise and talent. You need to have the structures we've talked about in place to allow room for the creativity to encourage the evolution of your company, all while keeping you on track and aligned.'

'I guess that's where RACI and being clear on boundaries and responsibilities will come into its own?'

'Precisely. Otherwise people will just turn up for work and stagnate or end up in a state of scope paralysis. You'll never scale at that rate. But your chances of doing so are hugely increased once your people are aligned to your vision, mission and values.'

Tom was beginning to make the links and see how they all fitted together, right back to us exploring personality types and how understanding the differences between people formed a fundamental ingredient of the Vaccine and underpinned each one of the five pillars. Having a scientific mind, Tom had discovered that the Leadership Vaccine was a practical solution to something that he'd thought was going to be an impossible problem.

'You know what?' he said 'I'm realising that my style of leadership is a product of people I used to report in to. And they really had no idea themselves what leadership was. I've had plenty of managers, but never a role model. And I guess they didn't either.'

As our time together ended for another day, I left Tom without defined homework this time. He had already agreed to use the RACI matrix across the organisation, and space, rest and time can be all we need to allow us to solidify our thoughts and make sense of new learnings. After all, he had plenty more work coming his way.

Summary

Leadership Vaccine Tenet Four:

CREATE the right organisational structure, not only in terms of the organisation chart itself, but also in terms of mindset, removing hierarchical constraints and ensuring empowerment of all team members.

Establish subject-matter expertise and accountability at all levels within the team.

With perfect clarity on culture and scope, Tom and his business were now ready to take on the third pillar of The Leadership Vaccine: structure. In terms of organisational structure, be that horizontal or vertical, it is important that an organisation chart exists that demonstrates how each and every person fits into the business, however we also need to define where responsibilities are delegated and where people are empowered to work within that structure.

A lot of leaders, like Tom, are afraid to let go of the old hierarchical systems of management and delegate more to their teams because they would still themselves be legally accountable if something went wrong. I explained to him how helpful a RACI matrix can be in this instance, making sure everyone in the business has clarity on who should take the lead in any given project. Tom was surprised to discover, as many leaders are, that he is actually an employee of his own business, and as such he needs to make sure the way he spends his time is of maximum value to the business. And spending his time doing tasks he could pay a team member a much lower salary to do is not of value at all.

Tom needs to realise that, just like the body doesn't have one T cell, it has millions, so that when one immune cell is attacked, the rest can survive, the business can't have one person taking control of everything. Instead, he needs to build in resilience by finding out which people in his teams are the right fit for each process. If people are just doing what they're told, the business will be missing a massive amount of knowledge, expertise and talent. He needs to have the structures in place to allow room for the creativity to encourage the evolution of the company while keeping it on track.

EIGHT

Inspire

16 January

By now, I am almost six months into my time with Tom, and each time we meet, I am seeing remarkable progress and results. Today was our first session of the New Year; people's resolutions were already history and long forgotten, much like the recent Christmas festivities themselves. Nevertheless, even on this cold, gloomy and damp January morning, it felt symbolic that I'd be exploring with Tom ways in which he could inspire and activate his teams. It felt like 'new beginnings', which was why Tom, like many of my clients, had naturally assumed that this was where we'd start the Vaccine process.

'Why did you think that?' I asked him.

'Because in my mind, if I could learn how to get my teams behind me and aligned to my way of working, then everything else would fall in place.'

'You mean if they showed you the respect you thought you deserved?'

'Ah, yes. Obviously, I can see where I got that all wrong! You only have to ask Ruth.' He laughed at his self-deprecation and I could see that he was already following my train of thought.

'And do they respect you?'

'Now, yes, of course they do.'

'What's changed?'

'One, I respect them, and two, I've earned it. That sounds really obvious now, but at the time, I couldn't see that at all. I thought you'd turn up, wave a magic wand, suggest a few incentive programmes, maybe an away day or two, and that would be it.'

'I can feel a "but" coming on...'

'But I know now that would've been like sticking a plaster over a really deep wound and hoping it would heal itself.'

'If only. Now you can see why we had to do a lot of the groundwork first before moving on to this stage of the Vaccine, starting with a thorough inspection of TBB's culture.'

'Oh God, don't remind me. I remember looking at you completely blankly. I had no idea what you meant, or how much I was influencing how bad things were.'

'I think "bad" is a bit strong, Tom. It was never bad, it just wasn't working for you or the business. And by that, I mean the people working in it. Your job as leader back then looked very different to the one that you do now. You've taken huge steps to fix the culture here and put in place systems and processes that work for everyone, you included. Once you began to focus more on your people, and recognised that different personality preferences needn't stop you from engaging with people who behaved or thought differently to you, you opened up new channels of communication and idea pathways from people you'd never actually spoken to before.'

'I know, look at Chris, and Linda. Especially Linda. She's taken on those twelve processes and turned three of them around into profit centres.'

'Exactly. That scoping exercise is one of the most important parts of my five pillars as it helps unlock people and profit before we look at structure. But you had to be open to your people first, and just as importantly, they to you.'

'It's a culture thing, isn't it? I can definitely feel the changes. It's a lot less lonely, for a start. I like it when people say hello to me when I walk in rather than shrinking behind their monitors. I like it even more that not everything rests on my shoulders. I've got some really excellent managers and group heads who want to bounce ideas around with me, and vice versa. I'm not the only one holding it all together the whole time, which I know was all down to me in the first place. This is why I'm excited to find out where we'll go with the staff-development part of your Vaccine.'

'Why does that excite you?'

'Simple. We now know what it is we do and who does what. I want to know how to support my teams to be the best versions of themselves so that they can continue to develop. We've given people roles they own, so I need to keep empowering them with the right tools and confidence. The thought of all that was a real headache for me before, but only because I didn't know how. Now, I'm ready.'

Sarah's story

I love this stage of the Vaccine because I get to see the value it delivers to leaders such as Tom in terms of understanding and embracing leadership. There's no single definition of that, of course, and it can change from one day to the next. Back in the day, I wish I'd had the benefit of The Leadership Vaccine, and I was envying seeing the weight dropping now from Tom's shoulders.

The need for inspirational development was exemplified in Tom's working relationship with Sarah. I'd noticed Sarah throughout my whole time at TBB; she'd attended the Team Strategy day and the personality preference workshop. Later, she was involved in the scoping exercise, but until recently, she'd remained an enigma to me because I couldn't work out her role and responsibility. Tom seemed to rely on her at every turn, although this was never explicitly expressed. Today, I asked for a quick chat with her to find out how she fitted into TBB and, more importantly, how she perceived her role.

As I'd imagined to be the case, Sarah had arrived as an administrator and, almost from day one, had supported Tom. Over time, her role had expanded organically, along with her list of responsibilities, and yet she didn't seem overly confident. I asked her how valued she felt, and how important she believed her role was, but she played this down.

'I'm just an administrator.'

'That might be how you started, but it's clear to me that you're not "just an administrator" anymore. I've seen you take control of your team and the processes you work with. In the workshops I've run, your input has been invaluable. You clearly know what you're talking about.'

Sarah was genuinely taken aback, as if this was the first time her contributions to the business had been acknowledged. The truth was, she had an extraordinary ability to build connections with people around her, both work colleagues and external business partners. I'd seen her turn potentially difficult conflict situations into ones filled with warmth and good humour.

That seemed to have passed Tom by completely, though. He viewed Sarah as a go-to dogsbody. It wasn't malicious on Tom's part; it stemmed from a sense of complacency that Sarah would always be 100% solid and reliable. Sarah was a prime example of why Tom now needed the staff-development pillar of The Leadership Vaccine because she was clearly an underrated, underappreciated co-worker with a great deal of skill and expertise who lacked the confidence to properly shine. In a culture where one-to-ones were not important, it was little wonder that Sarah considered herself to be 'just' an administrator.

One-to-ones

I knew that Tom hadn't been doing any one-to-ones at all. In fact, on my first site visit, I saw him casually cancel a meeting with a staff member in favour of handling a 'more important' matter instead. Now, of course, Tom was embarrassed when I reminded him of this.

My recommendation to Tom was that from now on, all line managers must hold monthly one-to-ones with everyone on their team, not only so that all the team members felt equally valued, but also because they'd be opportunities for the business to regularly feel the pulse of its employees and be aware of their needs and concerns. From Tom's face, I could tell he was already feeling outside of his comfort zone.

I was quick to reassure him.

'First off, remember these are times for you and your direct reports to have one-on-one discussions. I know that sounds obvious, but it's so important for the relationship between the direct report and the manager to be an open one. That requires having confidence and trust in each other, and the best way to build that is by spending time together. It's not just about having a chat. Of course, be human, but stay on point. Have a structure in mind and stay focused on the team member.'

'I'm glad you mention structure, that sounds more like me.'

'I generally use a template that I fill in with the notes I take to make sure we cover off a certain number of topics, such as workload, development or training needs, performance goals or objectives. And don't forget feedback.'

'This might be a strange question, but how do I start?'

'Start with an open question, like "How are you doing? How are you getting on? How are you finding things?" Doesn't matter whether the person has just arrived or been here twenty years, these questions work. Plus, it's a really nice way of opening the meeting informally and handing it over to them. What you're saying is, "This is about you," and that you're there to listen to what they have to say.'

'OK, so after they've told me everything I need to hear, how am I supposed to deliver feedback? It's the bit that worries me the most and probably why I've avoided one-to-ones in the first place.'

Feedback

I was glad Tom had raised this because giving feedback to a direct report can so often go horribly wrong.

'As a manager, it is your duty to have the courage to give constructive feedback in a timely fashion. Feedback isn't your opinion; it's fact-based, fair and transparent, and it's important to give it in a timely manner, such as in the privacy of regular one-to-ones. Nothing is worse than a direct report receiving negative feedback they didn't see coming during an end-of-year appraisal.

'When you offer feedback in a timely fashion, it gives both you and the direct report a chance to build strategies to improve performance, or to resolve any issues as they arise. Remember, though, feedback is a two-way street so you must invite the team member to offer feedback in return. You can do this by asking, "Is there anything more that I can do? How can we make this work even better?"'

'Okay this makes sense – so that's it?'

'Not quite. *Always* follow up the meeting. I would make a few notes, and at the end of the meeting I would generally send an email to my direct report to say it was great to meet with them, and here's a brief summary of what we talked about and some actions to take.

'Now, this is important. If you're talking about training needs and have suggested a course that you could look into for them, or maybe they want to do some job shadowing, you need to follow up on that commitment. Having a short, written summary and some notes that you share and agree on means that you can use them for the next meeting to make sure you're on track. So bottom line, remember these two things: it's their meeting, and make sure to follow up.'

Tom nodded. He'd been taking it all in and making notes.

'Like we're doing it together and this is what we've agreed, but structured?' he asked.

'Absolutely! Finally, whatever you do, *don't* postpone the one-to-one, unless it's absolutely necessary. And by that, I mean a dire emergency.'

Tom blushed; he knew he'd been guilty of fobbing people off in the past.

'Get all the one-to-ones in the diary as soon as possible, because people's diaries fill up quickly. If your direct report needs to talk to you and they've penned in time with you for that, maybe they're really concerned about a work issue, or they have a personal problem. If you then cancel or move that meeting, it can be quite stressful for them and that won't make them feel valued. On the other hand, if they want to move their one-to-one, that's OK if you can reschedule. If they want to cancel their one-to-one because they feel they don't have anything to discuss, I'd make sure you say to them, "Let's still catch up, even for ten minutes, just to have a chat." You don't want to get into the habit of losing one-to-ones.'

'You love one-to-ones, don't you, Rebecca!'

'Can you tell? And because I know how much you love structure, Tom, I'm going to give you a tool I like to use, called Co-Co plots.'

Co-Co plots

Tom's eyes lit up at the mention of this and he leant forward to look closely at the rough example I was sketching out. Using Sarah and one of her direct reports, Sam, as examples of two different profiles, I plotted how Sarah was highly experienced but lacking in confidence, whereas Sam was the complete opposite. I explained that Co-Co plots are based on ideas raised in *The Situational Leader* by Dr Paul Hersey,[13] and the Skill/Will plots described in the *Tao of Coaching* by Max Landsberg,[14] which I have adapted over the years of my using them with my teams.

In a Co-Co plot, competence (incorporating skill, knowledge and ability) is plotted on the x axis and confidence on the y axis.

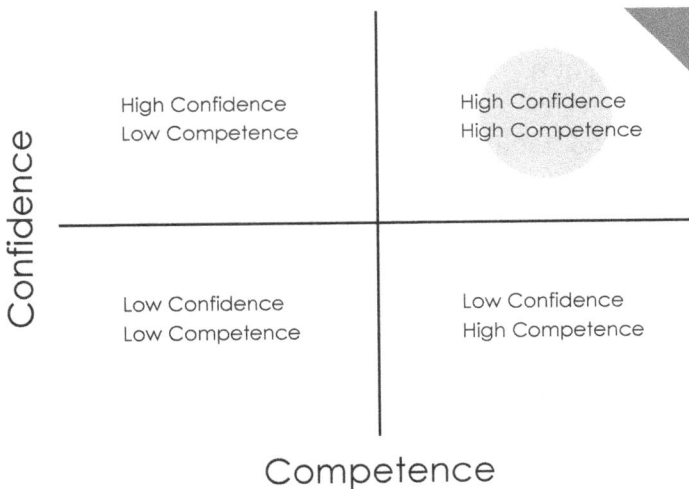

High Confidence Low Competence	High Confidence High Competence
Low Confidence Low Competence	Low Confidence High Competence

Confidence (y axis) — Competence (x axis)

---

13 P Hersey, *The Situational Leader* (Center for Leadership Studies Inc., 1984)

14 M Landsberg, *The Tao of Coaching: Boost your effectiveness at work by inspiring and developing those around you* (Harper Collins, 1996)

I explained how these plots work to Tom. 'When someone takes on a new task, they generally start in low competence, low confidence. As they train, they develop knowledge, skill and ability, so move along the x axis to high competence, low confidence. Once armed with this competency, they then practise. As they develop further capabilities and become more comfortable with the task, their confidence grows, and as a result they move up the y axis to high competence, high confidence. This is where we aim for all of our colleagues to be.'

'So, to move along the x axis, it's training, and to move up the y axis, it's practice?'

'You've got it.'

'What about the other box?'

'This box – high confidence, low competence – represents those situations where folks are super confident but may not have the competence. Again, to get them across that line into high competence, high confidence, it's training.'

I explained that the person is not in a box; it is each task. We can have a plot for an individual with some tasks in high competence, high confidence, newer responsibilities in the two lower boxes. This is where the magic happens as it allows us to bookmark new tasks that the team member may like to get involved with. Or, as we have seen in TBB's case, when new tasks are brought into the team as a whole, we can delegate them to an individual, being clear and understanding that we know they need training and the opportunity to practise. We aren't simply 'throwing it over the fence'.

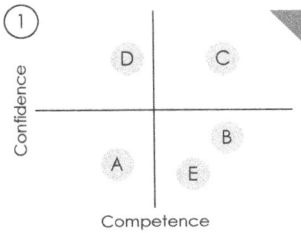

①

An example of an individual's Co-Co plot over the course of a year as tasks gradually move to high competence, high confidence. In (5), when all tasks are at or close to this ideal, new tasks may be introduced.

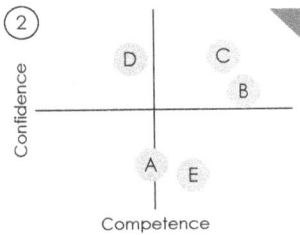

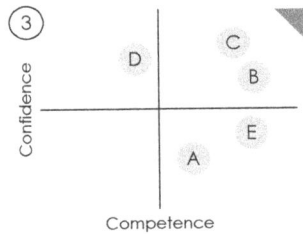

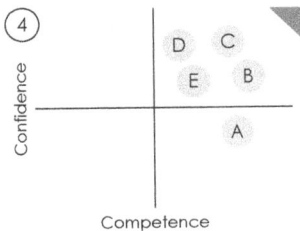

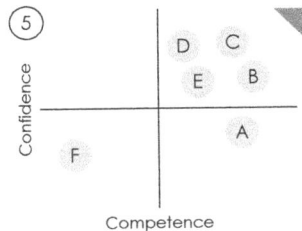

'That's absolutely fantastic!' Tom said. This structural, almost scientific approach was clearly appealing to his innate preference for managing projects and processes.

'Good,' I responded. 'The aim is to move towards high competence, high confidence for each individual's various responsibilities. At this point, you make an agreement with that person that for this task, you will step back, knowing they are fully competent and confident.

'At each step along the way, as they make progress on the plot with their tasks, you'll know the appropriate actions and approaches to adopt per individual per activity, as their line manager, to help them reach the high competence, high confidence point. For example, when they're low competence, low confidence, you need to be hands on for that task. If they're in high competence, low confidence for another task, don't keep training them for that process or activity, because it'll knock their confidence even more. They're already trained. At that point, give them a safe space to practise in.

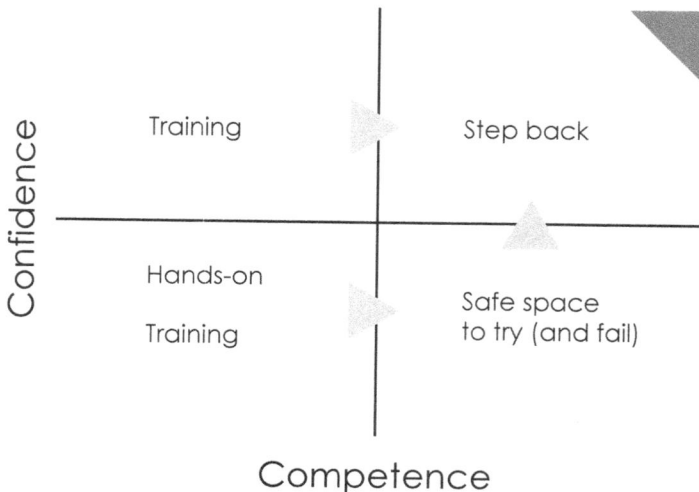

Confidence

Training | Step back

Hands-on Training | Safe space to try (and fail)

Competence

'What you've done in the past, when your colleagues have attained the high competence, high confidence level, was continue micromanaging them instead of stepping back and letting them get on with it, because you insisted on being so hands on. They felt like you didn't trust them enough, when in fact, they were more than competent.'

'You mean like Sarah?'

'Sarah's a case in point. She's at the high competence, low confidence point on the plot for many, if not all, of her responsibilities. What she needs is a safe space to practise where she can feel challenged. That's not going to happen unless you step back and stop treating her as "just" an administrator.'

A little respect

'And another thing...'

'Oh no, I can feel a telling off coming,' Tom said with a wry smile.

'Stop treating her like a dogsbody.'

'Do I?'

'I see so many leaders behave like this when they feel comfortable around certain people, like you do with

Sarah. Those "funny" little jokes that you don't aim at Rachel or David, or Chris even. Instead, you show them more deference and respect. Little things like that can really affect a team member's confidence levels. It's not intentional, just habit. But not a good one.'

'What do I need to do?'

'With Sarah, focus on how you can encourage her to take pride in where she is and what she contributes to TBB. Find ways for her to demonstrate to herself that she's able to do what she excels at without thinking you're constantly looking over her shoulder. She doesn't need your full-time approval; just let her realise that you know she's more than up to it, but you'll catch her if she falls.

'With Sam, on the other hand, look at his Co-Co plot and you can see he's all high confidence but low competence. He needs a conversation along the lines of, "We love your enthusiasm and want to continue to support you in getting to the high competence stage, but we don't think you are quite there yet." Even though that's a difficult discussion, because it's said in the positive context of partnering with him to aid his development, it's one that Sarah should be able to have with him because he reports directly into her. She needs her own confidence levels to rise so that she can effectively line manage him.

'But before that can happen, Tom, you need to sit down with Sarah and ask where she thinks she sits on the plot for each of her responsibilities. Help her raise her confidence so she can make the most of her knowledge. Then she'll be able to guide Sam better.

'If you apply this tool to everybody in the business on a monthly basis, then over the course of a year, you'll see people's tasks move along the plot as they train and become more confident. The most important point is reached when you, as line manager, can step back as your direct reports reach the high competence, high confidence level.'

This is why the staff-development pillar works best at this point in The Leadership Vaccine. For me, everything for a leader is about connection to their purpose, their people and the importance of their role. If Tom had dived straight into managing one-to-ones and drawing up Co-Co plots when I first met him, he'd still have no sense of overall direction for the business. He needed to first understand what his business and team were about.

It's vital that leaders have clarity on their direction, on the scope and boundaries of their role and responsibilities. Once they have that clarity, they can then build commitment not only to their shared goals, but also to each other and their customers. In TBB, everything that Tom had worked on so far regarding its culture, scope and structure had been designed to create connections and gain clarity. The result was that Tom was now in a strong position to essentially commit to his staff, having worked on identifying the valuable foundations of what made him tick.

When I first arrived, Tom himself was low competence, low confidence and didn't know how to lead. The process he'd since worked through had provided him with the right tools to build his leadership skills, preparing the ground for him to carry out the scoping exercise. This, in turn, had informed his perspective and vision of the company structure.

He'd also engaged with a more open and approachable attitude, and this had increased his confidence. In essence, I'd taken him through the same journey that he was aware his staff would need to take – people such as Sarah, with whom he now shared an empathy and outlook. It had made him even more acutely aware that TBB wasn't the vehicle that simply delivered 'The Tom Show' (to be fair, his lack of leadership skills were never driven by his ego, but the outcome was the same) because it was actually populated by a range of highly skilled subject-matter experts. His starring role should be more directed towards providing the right levels of support to help them, and the business, thrive and grow.

I asked him, if he were to stand in the middle of the office right now and share with the team what they could expect from him, what would he say? With remarkable alacrity, he didn't even blink. He spoke from the heart.

'I'm connected with you, we're all in this together. I want to demonstrate to you that as a leader, my focus is on you. This is who TBB is; this is what we do; this is what I need from you; this is your role and responsibility. You and I are going to work together so that you can fulfil that role and continue to grow onwards from that.'

I had to stop myself from giving him a round of applause, but I was genuinely delighted, and proud that Tom had come this far in a matter of a few months and could speak with such passion and clarity about his role and purpose in the company which, at one time, had been clouded by doubt and confusion. I knew that even as he and I parted company at the end of the Leadership Vaccine programme, Tom would still have conflicting priorities from time to time, but he would have a purpose, a vision and a mission to anchor him, and he would know how to prioritise with complete confidence. His colleagues would see these qualities in him, and they in turn would feel confident and inspired by his sense of commitment to both them and the business.

We all need a battle plan

Looking across the five pillars, some leaders will naturally be drawn to culture and staff development. Others will be drawn to scope, structure and process. The Vaccine's magic occurs when each and every area is attended to. We can't lead somebody into battle when we don't know what the battle is, who our cavalry is. If we don't have a battle plan in place, all that we're doing is riding a horse in the woods.

Entering battle can be an unsettling prospect, and I certainly saw that reaction in Tom when I said to him early on that, as a leader (be that of a team or a business), he was accountable and responsible for providing his staff with opportunities to develop while in his employ. My advice to Tom had always been that he needed all his colleagues to be energised, enthusiastic and inspired from day one, and not a crew of shipwrecked people who had to operate in a constant reactive state, feeling like they'd ended up in a dead-end job because nobody else wanted them, or that they couldn't lead their own teams – as had happened to some extent with Sarah. How refreshing it was to see all that starting to change within TBB. Tom was making all the connections we'd been working on the last few months and his newfound confidence was helping him become an inspirational leader.

The best way that Tom could inspire Sarah to develop her staff was to show her the benefits of being developed herself. Giving people ownership is ultimately what inspires them. It was a far cry from the Team Strategy day last year when Tom had no inkling that there were people working for him who had ideas of their own. He knew back then he wanted to scale, but he'd built a company that had outgrown itself and was in real danger of retracting unless something changed – and that had to be Tom.

Ruth asked me if I wanted yet another coffee, but it was almost the end of the day and there's only a certain amount of caffeine I can take. She'd been very attentive to us both all day, careful not to interrupt our flow. I got the sense that Ruth was also part of the magic that was happening in TBB. She'd always been a steadying influence on Tom, although I had to say, that was more in terms of gripping the steering wheel, trying to keep Tom on track. She had perhaps been his co-pilot, but never the driver.

These days, she had an air of deft authority about her, mixed with a kindness and compassion that was more obviously on show. When I'd had the chance, I'd sat and observed her working at her own station. Methodical, clear and efficient, she no longer seemed to be chasing, she was supporting.

I thanked her for everything she'd done today, especially for the great buffet lunch of salads and healthy wraps. Just up my street and in a different league to the prepacked cheese and onion sandwiches Tom had asked for six months ago.

Gathering up my belongings, I turned to Tom and asked, 'How are you finding this process now we've come this far?'

Tom suddenly looked a lot more serious than I'd expected. 'I honestly never realised how much time I spent worrying about how I was ever going to be a leader. Stressing about how on earth I'd ended up in this role. I didn't want this role – ask any of my friends, they'd back that up. I'm not somebody who'd ever be the leader of a group; I've always been quite happy to fade into the background. And then I started building TBB and had all these expectations. Honestly? It terrified me. But now I'm kind of excited because I can see that I can actually do this.'

'What's the best bit?'

'It so great to be a colleague again. I forgot how much I missed having teammates. When I was a technical leader, there were twenty-five other technical leaders I could be pals with. Now, I feel like I can come into work and I don't have to put on a brave face of supposedly knowing it all. I'm not the one constantly having to be on top of everything. I felt before like I didn't have time for my team, and then I'd get frustrated with them because they didn't understand that when they wanted my time, I was busy. Now, I can't even remember what it was like to be back there because I feel so much more hopeful.

'I know we've still got a load of work to do, but I believe I – we – can do this. Even if that means I'm not always going to get it right, at least I know I'm not always going to get it wrong.'

His words resonated with me deeply. I remembered that lonely place where I had the title of leader that I felt I didn't deserve or couldn't live up to. It constantly felt like at any moment everything could fall apart. Not only was I worrying about my own career, there were also the careers of all the people I was responsible for to worry about too. That pressure could be huge.

I remember going to dinner parties where there'd be friends of mine who held senior roles, and I'd be asking myself, 'How can you not be thinking about work all the time like I am?' Because it was all I ever thought about. I was never present when I was with my family or friends, and I constantly had a monkey on my back going, 'You're going to screw this up. It's all going to go wrong. You don't know what you're doing.' No wonder Tom used to look so tired every time we met when we began this process. These days, he looked like he got a lot more sleep.

Summary

Leadership Vaccine Tenet Five:

INSPIRE and activate your team by providing excellent staff-development opportunities so that the individuals within the team have not only the skills, but also the confidence to continuously improve themselves, their processes and their outputs.

Tom and TBB are ready to move on to the fourth pillar of the Leadership Vaccine, staff development. We start our first meeting of the New Year with a quick recap as to why the right culture had to be in place before we even touched on this. When he and I first met, Tom's teams didn't particularly respect him; they just robotically did as they were told. Now the feeling of mutual respect in the office is palpable.

The inspirational staff-development stage of the Vaccine is when we really see the value it delivers in terms of understanding and embracing leadership. I think particularly about Tom's attitude towards one member of his team, Sarah, whose skills and competence he has until now taken completely for granted. As a result, she feels unimportant and undervalued. Tom's inability to communicate his appreciation to Sarah heads us naturally on to the importance of one-to-ones. Although Tom feels uncomfortable with the idea at the moment, I remind him how important it is for the relationship between line managers and their reports to be an open one.

Tom's major concern with doing one-to-ones is the idea of giving feedback once the team member has had a chance to speak. I remind him that feedback must be fact based; it isn't simply his or a line manager's opinion. It also needs to be given on a regular basis, such as in a monthly one-to-one, rather than being stored up for the yearly appraisal. And of course, one-to-ones and the feedback from them must always be followed up with action. Finally, a leader must never cancel or postpone a one-to-one, otherwise they can make their reports feel undervalued. If the report wants to reschedule, that's fine, but no one should cancel a one-to-one completely.

To help Tom get comfortable with the idea of one-to-ones, I introduce him to a tool I have developed, based on ideas raised in the work of Dr Paul Hersey and Max Landsberg, called the Co-Co plot. This demonstrates how a team member moves from low competence, low confidence to high competence, high confidence as they get more used to completing a certain task, and it's in this latter quadrant of the plot that we want all our reports' tasks to be. Competence comes with training, confidence with practice. Once trained, a team member needs a safe space to practise the task until their confidence becomes as high as their competence.

NINE

Enable

10 February

First and foremost, as leaders we have a responsibility to our staff. When I returned to TBB, I was delighted when Tom told me that the one-to-ones had been going incredibly well. Both he and the line managers had been plotting out people's competence versus confidence, resulting in some positive discussions. I noticed the changes, seeing engaged and motivated people running with their processes. The whole place seemed energised by the personal challenges and successes that the teams were experiencing.

In particular, I noticed that both Sarah and Sam were flourishing in ways Tom could never have imagined, and that Chris's input and actions were making significant positive impacts on co-workers and clients alike. For Tom, this would be an ongoing evolutionary process. He fully accepted that, as leader, he was now able to step back in the knowledge that he had the structures in place to support the development of his direct reports, and they too had their own structures in place to develop *their* processes. It was almost as if he could breathe a daily sigh of relief because he'd effectively let go.

Subject-matter experts were beginning to feel like leaders in their own right. I was greatly encouraged to see that many of them were developing and documenting procedures when at one time, this was solely Tom's self-appointed responsibility. He now performed the role of reviewer and approver, together with his leadership team. This had allowed for the creation of additional standard operating procedures (SOPs) as well as a whole raft of practical and workable job aids, checklists and guides that were simply non-existent before the Vaccine programme. Today, Tom was able to view the business from a position of objectivity and consultative authority, as opposed to always digging himself out from its centre.

I also noticed a significant change in the vibe at TBB. At first, everyone, Tom included, seemed weighed down by crazily long to-do lists, when a priority was set only by taking a stab in the dark. Thanks to Tom's commitment towards making the changes, with complete buy-in from the team, those days were rapidly becoming a thing of the past.

Such had been Tom's progress through culture, scope, structure and staff development, I was ready to introduce him to the fifth and final pillar – process.

Gain oversight through a process inventory

It was only now that Tom was ready to begin compiling the definitive process inventory and understanding of what state each process was at. Having gone through the scoping exercise, he would find this much more straightforward than he would have done before. The first thing I did was to encourage Tom to ask his staff to prioritise the actions and tasks on their to-do lists (including their day-to-day activities) by categorising them into three 'buckets':

1. **Operate.** Operational tasks with the highest priority that have to be performed or completed to maintain, or re-gain, a state of compliance, be that with regulations or client expectations, or to deliver on contractual obligations. This category also includes tasks required for the functional day-to-day running of the business.

2. **Improve.** These are value-adding tasks or activities for processes or projects that are already compliant.

Improve tasks, increase or further improve the quality of those deliverables.

3. **Elevate**. Tasks that allow the business to operate at the highest levels of performance.

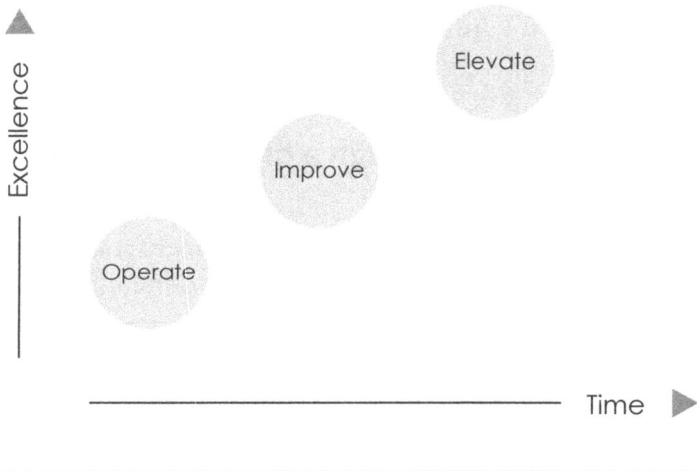

EXAMPLES FROM TBB

- Operate:
    - Submission to client of project design
    - Project execution activities
    - Responding to questions from regulators
    - Writing of an SOP required as part of a regulated process that is lacking in the quality management system
    - Performing one-to-ones
- Improve:
    - Update of an SOP to improve readability
    - Project relating to improvement of how quality metrics are being presented

- Update of pitch deck for business
- Process improvement projects
- Costing review of external vendors
- Elevate:
  - Speaking at an industry conference
  - Update of brochure to add new photographs
  - Rebranding of company logo
  - Writing thought leadership pieces for industry magazine

I often find that if individuals don't actively prioritise, their attention can head straight towards the 'sexier' bucket marked 'elevate'. Of course, we all need that to help raise our visibility and profile, but if more urgent matters need attention to maintain our clients', regulators' or companies' expectations, then they absolutely must take priority.

Once individuals' to-do lists and daily activities are categorised, we follow this by establishing a process inventory that includes all the various tasks that sit underneath each main process. This builds transparency and offers a clear-sighted view on what is, and isn't, a priority, and how each sub-process links to one another.

'This will allow you to see clearly what is going on within the business, without you having to spend hours on creating that inventory yourself,' I said to Tom.

'I'm all ears. How?'

'By putting a call out to all your subject-matter experts and asking them and their teams to create a list of the processes, tasks, actions and activities they perform, categorise each into operate, improve and elevate and then populate these into a master database. They already have their to-do lists and the tasks listed from the recent scoping exercises, so this should be relatively easy to now do.

'There are many different programs available to choose from for this master database, even something as simple as Microsoft Project.[15] You see immediately what's going on in each process and where the highest priority actions and tasks are. It also has the added advantage of allowing you to link this to your quality management system so you can see what documents you have in place to support each task, and what metrics you're gathering to oversee them.'

'I'm guessing that'll show us all exactly where we're focusing our energies and inputs?'

'And it'll prompt everyone to ask *why* you're working on some tasks instead of chasing the monsters out from underneath the bed.'

'There have been a few of those, that's for sure.'

'Except now, you're discovering what they are and where they lurk. The main thing is to not be frightened of

---

15   www.microsoft.com

confronting them. Hold them up to scrutiny. Otherwise, they'll gnaw away at your foundations, the cracks will appear, and clients will walk away. You've already seen that happening at TBB.'

'It's one of the things that's kept me awake at night, not knowing how to stop that.'

'That was because you lacked the framework to prioritise, and you didn't trust people working on the processes enough to do the job for you. They also knew you didn't trust them. So, let me ask you, if there's one part of a process that sits in the elevate bucket, but an interlinking process sits in operate, which one do you think should take priority?'

'Operate, obviously. Without that, it's impossible to achieve excellence.'

'Exactly. Stepping back and mapping the overarching landscape lets you see where risks are before they become issues and work out what needs to be prioritised to achieve and maintain compliance in the comfort of knowing that resources are being deployed effectively. That then leads to you being in a position to improve the way you work, and finally achieve excellence. Put simply, it's a case of walking before running.

'It also allows you to see how tasks inter-rely on each other. Are there areas where you need to adjust boundaries? Don't forget, you've already done the scoping exercise, so you know what activities you have to do.

This is more about the nitty gritty of the order in which you're going to do them.'

'Presumably the one-to-ones will help with this as we can use that time to check in rather than watching over team members' shoulders,' said Tom, piecing the whole picture together.

'Absolutely. The key thing here is that the team members themselves prioritise, line managers can challenge if they truly disagree, but let the team members have the first stab at prioritising, as this will allow them to own their prioritisation. One-to-ones then give the opportunities for managers to challenge their direct reports if needed: "I know you really want to work on this part of the process because it excites you, but remember you've put that in the elevate bucket. We need to look at these compliance issues first, otherwise we'll risk not meeting our customers' service level agreements." Now that your teams own what they do, this gives them clarity on why they do it. Also, it allows you to capture great ideas and innovations even when there isn't time to work on them at the moment. You can capture them in the elevate bucket, firstly ensuring that you don't forget the suggestions but also so that the person who raises the idea isn't demotivated by being simply told, "It's not possible", but rather, "It is possible, just not right now while there are operate tasks to complete."'

Sarah was solid evidence of the transformation within TBB. It was clear she was a subject-matter expert leading a team of other subject-matter experts, and that she had so much more confidence now. Tom was showing more deference and respect towards her in meetings. Sarah was flourishing and developing world class processes with her team. She'd prioritised a set of operate actions and, as she told me animatedly during a coffee break, she would no longer had sleepless nights worrying about her own monsters under the bed because her priorities would be properly mapped out.

As The Leadership Vaccine took hold, Tom could step back more with complete confidence, knowing that he had excellent and talented staff who had chosen to build their careers at TBB. Tom's emerging role as an inspiring leader was helping to develop a highly motivated, aligned team of people who would actively rise to solving challenges instead of reluctantly accepting them as part and parcel of the job. If somebody fell sick, the others pulled together and looked to see what was on that person's to-do list, which now had visibility. If somebody left the company, it would be easy to identify what processes they were working on and transfer them across to another skilled team member.

Transparency across the organisation also meant it was building resilience. For Tom, it changed everything. When we first met, the problems in the business were eating into his profit, thus stalling his plans to scale, and the business was at risk of retracting. He couldn't see any way of turning his ship around and everyone, himself included, lacked a coherent sense of identity and purpose.

What the business had lacked was a leader who could connect all the dots and ensure alignment. Today, he could clearly articulate what his company was and the direction it was heading, supported by a rigorous set of standards and quality management systems. Furthermore, he could confidently state that the business would continue to grow and become increasingly resilient.

The reason the Vaccine enables staff to develop robust end-to-end future processes is *because* they're developed, owned and tested by the front-line people who work with them, not just the leader and a small clique. With subject-matter experts empowered to own their processes, Tom no longer needed to be solely responsible for monitoring numerous changes in legislation, since he could rely upon the experts he'd employed. They could attend conferences, read the industry press, have their ears to the ground to listen and learn about what was around the corner. They could prioritise actions to prepare for changes in regulations. Tom was no longer the knowledge bottleneck and didn't need to spend hours working well below his pay grade. His role was to oversee and to review (when necessary), not do – after all, he was the A in the RACI.

Company morale improves as a result of people feeling more trusted and empowered. Imagine the difference it would make to a junior member of staff to be named as the author of a process with the approval from the leader. In my own experience, the opportunity to play a part in my staff's development and career progress has been by far the most rewarding feeling I've experienced as a leader. Seven months into the Vaccine, I was seeing Tom appreciate this reward as he inspired the other leaders he needed. That is the foundation of leadership.

KPIs

Defining KPIs to measure key milestones throughout a process further allows leaders to identify risks before they become compliance issues. For example, as per TBB's service level agreements (SLAs), project scoping reports were delivered to clients within ninety days of kick off. The goal wasn't simply to measure the success of delivering the report to the client by day ninety. Yes, of course that was important, but not everything. It was about taking close consideration of each of the timelines within that process, governed by the process documentation.

The TBB SOP required background data to be gathered by day fifteen for review and processing by day thirty. The document was drafted by day sixty, and then sent out for quality control and internal review. At the moment, the day fifteen data gathering time point was consistently missed, with team members constantly playing catch up to meet the day ninety deadline. This might not have been an SLA noncompliance issue, but the risk if it persisted was that one day, TBB wouldn't be able to catch up later in the process and as a result would miss day ninety. Consequently, Tom and his teams would have an SLA non-compliance, and a potentially unhappy new client, on their hands.

In addition, the need to catch up time impacts any team's ability to plan, and it's my strong view that planning leads to efficiency. Also, squeezing later time points may not leave enough time for due care and attention to ensure that the project is not only delivered on time, but is also of high quality. By identifying that risk in advance – through a robust set of KPIs, which are reviewed by process owners, not simply SLA compliance metrics – teams can head the need to squeeze time later off at the pass and ensure that any inherent issues can be rectified without risking SLA or regulatory deadline compliance.

Root cause analysis

In TBB's case, the delay in delivering the data had been put down to a lack of training. Over the years, as a signatory on non-compliance reports in a number of organisations, I have so often heard this being put forward as the cause of an issue. Each time I challenge and dig further to get to the root of the problem. Training and retraining rarely solve the problem if we don't fully understand why the training wasn't rolled out to the right individuals or wasn't sufficient in the first place.

Back at TBB, I challenged Tom:

- Were people not clear on how to gather the data?

- Was data not being supplied in a timely manner?

- Were there checks and balances in place to prevent these delays from consistently occurring?

Sadly, Tom had no reasonable explanation. His solution had been to offer retraining in the processes, without actually getting to the root causes of the problems.

I remember one of my leaders in the past saying, 'People don't make mistakes, processes do.' That is so true. We always need to accept a certain degree of human error will occur, especially in smaller businesses where not everything is automated; however, the process should be designed with the appropriate checks and balances in place to ensure that such errors cannot easily be made, and certainly not consistently made.

At TBB when I'd first arrived, morale had been low and teams were facing an increasing number of difficult compliance issues. Team members blamed lack of training, Tom blamed the people, and no one seemed to blame the true root causes. With hindsight, Tom could see the value of asking why to delve deep into the real reasons the business had faced so many compliance issues. For example:

- People were not following the processes.

- Why? Because they weren't committed to the processes.

- Why? Because they weren't involved in the discussion to create them.

- Why? Because Tom wrote all the processes and they determined what everyone did.

- Why? Because Tom wanted to be involved in everything.

- Why? Because Tom didn't have confidence in his staff.

- Why? Because Tom didn't have confidence in himself as a leader.

What was the root cause of TBB's compliance issues? Without wanting to sound too harsh, one could see how many, if not all, stemmed from Tom and his approach to leadership.

This is just an example. I'm not suggesting that every non-compliance is a leadership issue. Often there are other issues at play.

HOW DEEP TO DELVE

The aim of this example is to show you how deep you need to delve to be confident that you really understand what caused the issue. Keep asking why – some might say like my three-year-old, Theo; others might reference Sakichi Toyoda, who developed the '5 Whys' tool which was used in the Toyota production system in the early twentieth century, where teams were encouraged to ask why five times to get to the root of the issue – until you get there.[16]

There are many root cause analysis techniques that add to this concept. You can Google 'The 5 whys', 'Fishbone analysis' or 'the 5Ms'. In this book, I just wish to encourage you not to take issues at face value. Make sure you scratch below the surface, looking for the true root cause.

Developing CAPA plans

Having a series of measurable KPIs in place, we have the chance to investigate and resolve any process issue or risk before it becomes a live compliance issue. It will also represent a huge shift from the days of only focusing on the 'drop dead' date to the regulator or the client. In focusing on all of the steps leading up to that point, we ensure the end delivery date almost takes care of itself.

At TBB, for example, Tom would only need to ask, 'How's process X going?' If there were no issues, he wouldn't need any further information. If an issue arose because staff hadn't been following the process correctly, further investigation might suggest that the

---

16   T Ohno, 'Ask "Why" Five Times about Every Matter' (2006), www.toyota-myanmar.com/about-toyota/toyota-traditions/quality /ask-why-five-times-about-every-matter

process, or the team member's role within it, wasn't clear. Deeper still, it might be that the system in use was too cumbersome, which encouraged teams to fall into a less-than-desirable workaround solution. Just like water, people will always find the easiest way.

Only by thoroughly understanding the root cause of an issue can we develop an effective corrective and preventive action (CAPA) plan. Such plans have a number of distinct sections with associated outcomes or actions:[17]

1. Root cause analysis – our investigation with the 5 whys, 5Ms or other similar tool, resulting in us being able to articulate the ultimate root cause of the issue at hand.

2. Correction – 'action to eliminate the detected non-conformity'. What needs to be done to fill the gap or correct the issue, e.g. rework.

3. Corrective action – 'action to eliminate the cause of a nonconformity and to prevent recurrence'. What action will be taken, by whom and in what timeline, to correct the *cause* of the issue and prevent it from happening again.

4. Preventive action – 'action to eliminate the cause of a potential nonconformity or other potential

---

17 International Standard ISO 9000, *Quality management systems – Fundamentals and vocabulary* (2015, fourth edn)

undesirable action'. What action will be taken, by whom and in what timeline, to prevent a *potential* issue from occurring. This applies when something is caught ahead of becoming an issue, e.g. a near miss.

5. Effectiveness checks – what checks will be implemented to assure us that the CAPA was effective.

Wherever possible a CAPA plan should be developed, reviewed and approved in advance of actions taking place, and be tracked to ensure its commitments are being completed in a timely manner. Only when the effectiveness checks have been completed should a CAPA be considered closed.

I recommend using CAPAs not only for regulatory or SLA non-compliance issues, but also for business issues, e.g. client complaints, as much as possible. This means that fixes are planned, approved and ultimately implemented, being tracked the whole way through to ensure we are taking thoughtful rather than reactive action.

As a senior leader, I've made mistakes and I've needed to write complex CAPA plans using a variety of root cause analysis tools. To be honest, while none of us like making mistakes, it's not the end of the world. It's not about how we make a mistake; it's how we come back from that mistake. If we need to contact a client to admit that we have made mistakes, but we've conducted a thorough investigation, and going forward, a series of checks and balances will be in place that will be monitored for effectiveness in the coming months, then chances are that client will be happy because we've shown what a safe pair of hands we are. This can only be achieved within a culture where people can, and will, speak up without fear. And in highly regulated industries, the stakes are simply too high to ignore this.

Summary

Leadership Vaccine Tenet Six:

ENABLE your team to develop robust, efficient and future-proofed end-to-end processes with enhanced oversight where issues and risks are identified early, mitigated proactively and lead to robust improvements.

With the one-to-ones in place and going well, and all the tasks mapped out on Co-Co plots, Tom and his team members are feeling energised and confident. Tom's reports now feel able to create their own processes, a formerly self-appointed task that fell solely on Tom's shoulders, freeing up yet more of his time. Such has been Tom's progress through culture, scope, structure and staff development, I'm ready to introduce him to the fifth and final pillar – process.

The first thing I encourage Tom to do is to categorise all tasks and actions into one of three 'buckets': operate, improve and elevate, warning him not to fall into the trap of concentrating on the 'sexy' elevate bucket. He can facilitate this by asking his subject-matter experts to create a list of their processes, tasks, actions and activities to populate a master database. They already have their to-do lists and the tasks listed from the recent scoping exercises, so this should be relatively easy to do.

With priorities mapped out and complete clarity and visibility on everyone's tasks and priorities, Tom can step back with confidence that he has a team of skilled and aligned people working with him. If someone is absent, or a team member leaves, this clarity makes it a simple process to pass their tasks on to another team member.

The reason the Vaccine enables staff to develop robust end-to-end processes is because they're owned and tested by the front-line people who work with them. Company morale improves as a result of people feeling more trusted and empowered. Seven months into the Vaccine, Tom is appreciating the reward of inspiring the other leaders he leads. That is the foundation of leadership.

Defining KPIs to measure key milestones throughout a process allows leaders to identify risks before they become compliance issues. For this the goal isn't simply to measure the success of the process by the final delivery metric; it's about close consideration of each of the timelines within that process, governed by the process documentation. Seeing how well a process is working allows us to head off risks *before* they result in compliance issues.

When compliance issues do occur, leaders can often assume they occur due to a lack of staff training, without having the correct discussions to discover the true root cause. Remember, people don't make mistakes, processes do. Keep asking why until you get to the real root cause of the problem. Only by thoroughly understanding the root cause of an issue can you develop an effective CAPA plan.

A CAPA plan should be developed, reviewed and approved in advance of actions taking place, and be tracked to ensure its commitments are being completed in a timely manner. Only when the effectiveness checks have been completed should a CAPA be considered closed.

TEN

Execute

So often, I see leadership strategists and management consultants walk into businesses either to help build them from scratch, or with a mission to rebuild. Once that task is complete, they walk out the door, only to return to the same business a few years later to rebuild it because it has lost its way and steered (back) off course.

The Leadership Vaccine is engineered to counteract this cyclical pattern of build and decay, being designed to empower leaders so that they can continue to monitor and regularly adjust their course if needed, instead of trying to turn the *Titanic* at full steam ahead (and we all know how that ended). By reviewing the system regularly, leaders will find that the adjustments to the course don't need to be significant. Simply a nuance or nudge in one direction will keep it on track. That's when we see the Vaccine begin to take its full effect.

My task with TBB over the last eight months had been to inject this methodology into Tom's mindset to empower him to steer his course with complete confidence. During that time we'd moved through the five pillars and administered the Vaccine in doses, constantly reviewing progress together. When I left Tom at the end of the previous chapter, he was looking at the process of supporting the team and any non-compliances with a wholly proactive approach. I recommended to him that by the time he reached the twelve-month anniversary of the start of the programme, the business should carry out its first review, and then on a regular basis every six to nine months a) to ensure the teams are still on course, b) to ask if everything is still fit for purpose and c) to check with the teams to see if they remain invigorated and excited.

Tom agreed this was a necessary step forward for him as a leader, but also in respect of the holistic development of TBB. As a result of the Vaccine, he'd already seen tangible positive results in performance and efficiencies, and in increased profit margins directly related to incremental improvements. In an email, I checked in to see how he was getting on and asked him if he felt any more confident in his abilities to steer this ship of his, and his instant response was, 'Absolutely.' I wished him well and told him that I would be back in July to monitor progress.

The one-year anniversary

25 July

I was delighted to be back in the now familiar and happy surroundings of TBB to see Tom and the team, reminding me of how hot this day last year was when poor Tom had been under mounting pressure. Today as I met Tom, he was like a different man altogether. Nowadays he seemed younger than his forty-one years, and much lighter than the man I'd met before the Team Strategy day last year.

As usual, we made small talk, but this time Tom's chat was all about what was going on in the teams and their achievements, and his two children, Poppy and Mac. I'd always known he had kids, but this was the first time I was hearing all about them and their shared holidays, weekends and days out. I cannot tell you how happy I was to see Tom so happy and relaxed. It would seem that he had grabbed some life for himself and his family back from the grasps of TBB.

After a lovely catch up, lasting almost an hour, we got back to the business of the day. Today I wanted to work with Tom in creating the framework for the rec-ommended regular reviews. One concept I wanted to introduce was including both annual and mid-year *team* appraisals in addition to the individual staff appraisals. Sadly, such team reviews aren't usual practice in many organisations, but I wanted Tom to embed this as a regular exercise to sustain the positive changes he and his teams had already achieved and to lead to further positive changes in the future. It would also be an opportunity for Tom to revisit each of the five pillars.

Culture

When revisiting the first pillar of the Vaccine, culture, we wanted to know from everyone in the business if they were still:

- Living and driving towards the vision
- Living their mission every day
- Living their values
- Feeling connected to the vision, mission and values

I wanted Tom to be completely up to speed on what happens when new people join the company. Are they being offered holistic onboarding so that they feel that they have a stake in TBB's future? Do they understand that the vision and mission are not just phrases on a slide, but within the day-to-day culture of TBB they actually have context and meaning?

Overall, Tom needed to be sure that the business is still on track. If it's not, why not? For example, if team members are not living their mission, should Tom be asking whether the mission statement itself was right in the first place? This is the whole point of this first review being a few months after we'd completed the last pillar to allow things to settle in.

When I asked Tom for his impressions so far, he looked a little uncomfortable before saying, 'Of the values we identified all those months back, all of us are finding that "boldness" isn't resonating as we'd hoped.'

'Do you know why that's the case?'

'No. Nobody seems to be able to put their finger on it.'

I suggested he arrange to send out an anonymous staff survey asking everyone for their views on the company's mission, vision and values. I wanted him to also dig deeper and ask:

- Are they clear on what their job entails?

- How do they feel about their autonomy?

- Do they feel they are offered enough support, and if so, is it the right level of support?

I also suggested he survey TBB customers to gauge how they were finding the new levels of service and company communication and if there were areas that could be improved upon.

10 August

Two weeks later when the staff survey results were back, I returned to TBB. It was interesting to discover that overall, the results were highly positive, but Tom's concerns were correct: boldness as a value wasn't resonating. I proposed to Tom that perhaps the underlying value was relevant, but the phrase wasn't. I suggested that each team leader select one of the values and a team member to deliver a TEDx style talk to the group, just a few minutes in length, during which they could explore in depth the meaning of that value.

Often values simply mean what the senior leader says they mean, but in reality, 'boldness', for example, could represent any one of twenty different things to twenty different people. I explained to Tom that my advice was a means of reaching consensus where a value would then become embedded and spring to life. He should then repeat the survey to determine if the number of values needed reducing from five to four. If so, that would keep them alive and fresh, as opposed to abstract and muddled.

Having received responses to his customer survey, Tom was most definitely buoyed and glowing with pride. The feedback regarding communication and expertise was highly positive. Customers felt cared for, and they hugely appreciated having a named member of staff to contact when the need arose. This was really encouraging for Tom because it showed that distributed control was working effectively now that subject-matter experts had been defined and put in place. A couple of clients still reported some continuing non-compliance issues, but for these issues, corrective measures were well underway. They would just take a little time to complete, purely down to the nature of the issues.

The feedback suggested that customers were confident TBB had its issues under control and was implementing the relevant corrective and preventive measures. Tom wasn't exactly thrilled that some customers were still experiencing problems, so I reassured him that he was making great progress and there was light at the end of the tunnel. The important takeaway was retaining customers' continued confidence and being further ahead than he was twelve months ago.

Customers were responding well to Tom's greater levels of transparency, which had come about as a direct result of him absorbing the Vaccine. As I said to him, 'If you hadn't embraced this process with an open mind, there was a real danger that some of those clients might have fallen away. Or worse still, initiated some form of action against you.'

'You're right. I just want it all to be perfect from now on.'

'Then I've got news for you, Tom, there's no such thing as perfect, especially when it comes to leadership. People are inspired by how you deal with failure just as much as they are by your success. It makes you human. Don't kid yourself: not everything's going to be perfect here, and nobody should expect that.

'Part of living up to the values of the business is in facing challenges. At one time, you'd have tried to sort it out all on your own, but that was getting you nowhere. Now, you've got a whole team behind you. Just look at the survey results. The fact that people are saying boldness doesn't resonate with them is a successful outcome. It shows they feel they can express their opinions honestly. There was a time you'd never even have bothered to ask. Who wants to be surrounded by a bunch of yes people anyway? The culture at TBB has changed.'

Scope

When Tom and I reviewed scope, I could see some creep had occurred. What I now invited Tom to do was to focus on the new elements that had been added and challenge why they'd been added.

'Is it because of legislation? Or because you realised there was a missed opportunity?'

Tom looked a little sheepish and blushed as he replied. 'Ah yes, that was one thing the client really needed and we said we'd do it. Sort of.'

'That's fine, but what's the extended opportunity with this process? The reason I ask – and I know you know this by now – is because if you are going to add to your scope, your business needs to continue to evolve. Is this aligned to your purpose, and if so, are you fully leveraging this new process? Have you offered it out to other clients?'

'It is aligned, but we hadn't considered offering it out to others.'

'But that's crazy, isn't it? If client X wants it and you plan on delivering it, shouldn't you be thinking whether you can scale it and offer it to other clients? You don't want to get into that same old situation again where you're taking on too many different processes just to keep one or two clients happy. This is when you decide if you need to keep it, in which case you work out how you can leverage it and take on the extra task of training people in a new process. Put it on your website, tell the world you've got a new offering and market the hell out of it. Adjust.'

Structure

I was over the moon to see that in respect of this pillar, TBB was looking fantastic now that all the subject-matter experts were in place. I made a point of asking Chris, David, Sarah and Sam how each was getting on, and when I told Tom their responses, his face was a picture.

It had never occurred to him that people could actually respect him for *not* being the centre of TBB's universe, but everybody I spoke to seemed really pleased that he'd been able to step back and admit that he'd not been good at delegating. His entire team now reported that they felt trusted and confident that Tom had put in place the right structure, and they all now had greater clarity on their roles and place within the organisation, as did their teams.

Staff development

Until Tom began The Leadership Vaccine, this pillar had been, sadly, pretty non-existent. A central foundation of the business had been missing, so today I was delighted to learn that the line managers were holding regular one-to-ones and sharing their notes with their direct reports. I was also pleased they'd been using the Co-Co plots to support colleagues' progression.

This was the area that received the most positive feedback in the staff survey. People were genuinely thrilled that they were being viewed as individuals and not simply being trained, trained, trained as if they were robots. Line managers were taking the time and space to ask staff meaningful questions about their opinions in addressing any issues that arose. As a result, an overall sense of partnership existed between them.

Process

With the processes, most of the quality management system documents had been re-written and streamlined, the vast majority initiated and led by colleagues outside of the leadership team. There had also been an increase in CAPA plans because more issues had been identified through this process. With the more open culture, these issues were being raised to management without hesitation. There were no more monsters under the bed and there was a huge sense of relief all round that people knew what they needed to deal with on a daily basis. Furthermore, they could manage these tasks in an orderly and aligned way.

To test this, I spoke with a recent new recruit, Angela, who'd joined TBB since the Vaccine programme had been implemented. Angela is a senior subject-matter expert, but not a line manager. Her role is to leverage and serve one of the extra core processes that emerged from the original scoping exercise, and I was keen for Tom to discover what her impressions of TBB were so far.

I asked Angela:

- How do you feel about your onboarding process?

- Are you clear on the vision, mission and values of TBB?

- Do you feel like you belong?

Tom was a little nervous before we asked her into the conference room, as this was the litmus test for how well he was really doing. Throughout her interview, Angela talked about how she enjoyed the culture and the open style of leadership at TBB. She also commented that, as much as she loved her last place of work (a close rival to TBB), this was the first time she'd felt trusted on account of her subject-matter expertise, and this had boosted her confidence. Angela also felt that she could be open and honest in asking for more training or practice when she needed it, and she said that the Co-Co plot discussions with her manager made her feel comfortable in requesting help in the knowledge she would be supported, without fear of having a task taken away from her.

Tom couldn't have been more delighted with Angela's appraisal.

His relationship with Chris had also never been better. Yes, they still challenged each other, but now they laughed when they did so, because they knew what to expect from each other. The vibe in TBB had definitely changed for the better, and as a regular visitor myself, I was greeted warmly by everyone I said hello to when I arrived.

Tom was now feeling that the business was in a much better position to seek external investment, but interestingly, he wasn't sure whether that was the route he wanted to pursue, given the company's improved performance. Unlike twelve months ago, he could see profitability returning and the business wasn't retracting after all. Only one client had gone by the wayside, but in terms of the newly defined scope, it was a client he could afford to let go.

'It was a scar we needed to get,' he observed.

'That's true,' I told him. 'You can't vaccinate against everything. Sometimes we need to feel the pain to understand the importance of what we're doing.'

Then Tom really took me by surprise with what he said next.

'You know what? I'm actually taking a holiday. Afterwards, that's when I'll decide what I'm going to do. I still have all my plans to scale for the future, but the difference now is that I feel like I have a choice. That's such a great feeling, because I never thought I'd get to this point in a million years. The most rewarding thing is knowing that people really want to work here and that they're proud to work here. They're not just pushing through the day, counting down the clock until they can knock off; they are actually thriving.'

'Don't forget, you're thriving, too. It's proof that you're a leader. Look at you: you're not holed up in your office. Your door is open to everyone.'

As if on cue, Sam popped his head in and said, 'Hey, Tom, I'm heading to Subway, fancy anything?'

Sam might as well have given Tom a million quid because the look on his face said it all.

After Sam had bounced back into the main office to take more orders from his team, Tom beamed and said, 'A year ago, nobody would ever have asked me that.' For me, that summed up one of the biggest changes in TBB. Tom is respected because his colleagues choose to follow him. You can't make someone follow you. When Sam checked in with Tom and asked, 'Hey, do you want a Subway?' he knew he'd cracked it. It meant his teams would also be willing to say, 'Hey, I need some help.'

My job was almost done. Tom looked disappointed when I told him that.

'Don't worry,' I reassured him, 'I'll always be available on the end of the phone, and I'll check in to see how you're getting on, but this is up to you now. You can do it. Just don't forget you are a leader first, technician second. Keep working together with your teams and keep up your regular system reviews. It's great to see you like this, but I want to see you like this in three years, in five years, in ten years. Probably by then your mission statement will have changed, but your vision, probably not, because it's such a big, audacious goal. But you have to continue with the Vaccine, and you have to keep bringing people along with you. Just like you've done with Chris and Sarah, Sam and Angela. Will you commit to that before I go? Can you do this?'

'Well, if I don't do this, I'll end up back where I was, so I'm bloody well going to do it.'

'Great, because this is where I hand the reins over to you.'

Summary

Leadership Vaccine Tenet Seven:

EXECUTE regular reviews to ensure ongoing team development and re-setting as needed.

Too often, businesses get help to build or rebuild effectively, only to fall back into the old ways and need rebuilding again a few years later. The final tenet of The Leadership Vaccine, execute, takes us beyond the pillars and mitigates this risk. By reviewing the system more regularly, leaders will find that the adjustments to the course don't need to be significant.

When I left Tom at the end of the fifth pillar of the Leadership Vaccine, he was looking at the process of supporting the team and any non-compliances with a wholly proactive approach. I recommended then that he needed to review the process twelve months after he'd first started it, then every six to nine months.

With that in mind, in July, I am back at TBB for the first review.

One concept I want Tom to introduce are annual and mid-year *team* appraisals in addition to the individual staff appraisals at TBB. This regular exercise would sustain the positive changes Tom and his teams have already achieved and lead to further positive changes in the future. It would also be an opportunity for Tom to revisit each of the five pillars:

- Culture
- Scope
- Structure
- Staff development
- Processes

Later, as Ruth walks with me to the main doors on the ground floor, I ask her out of curiosity how life in the office feels to her these days.

'Oh, things are completely different, and that includes Tom. Did he tell you he's actually taking a week's holiday with his family at the end of the month? This is unheard of.'

'He did, and I'm really pleased for him. Is he going to be on call, or is anyone standing in for him?'

'Chris is standing in, of course.'

Ruth and I exchange a smile in recognition that this would never have happened just a few months ago.

'What about you?' I ask.

'Oh, I'm going on holiday, too, and this time, I won't be taking my office mobile. Tom's told me that when he's gone, he's gone. I share all my notes with Chris's PA, Shona. She can handle anything urgent that comes my way.'

I'm genuinely thrilled for Ruth. Of all the people I've met at TBB, Ruth has perhaps been the most committed to Tom through thick and thin and has often been his go-to emergency button. It regularly left Ruth with little time to herself to gather her own thoughts or manage her top-heavy workload. Now, even Ruth has been able to work through her own processes, share with her peers and speak with Tom about the challenges she is facing. Things have really looked up for Ruth each time they have for Tom.

Ruth and I shake hands as we part, both pausing and smiling as we realise we have never done that before.

Conclusion

I wonder how many of you have started to imagine what Tom looks like, where he might have worked in the past and what university he went to. I feel like I know Tom as an individual. I can even picture who would play him in a movie!

Tom is, in fact, all of us.

The reason Tom is not a 'real' person,[18] and that this is not a specific case study, is because when we look at real individuals, we form our own impressions and, dare I say it, we have our own biases. Whereas with a fictious composite, I was able to get straight down to the facts, rather than examining in detail the personality.

---

18 In case you missed my earlier footnote, yes, Tom is not real!

My guess is that certain aspects of Tom have given you the punch-in-the-gut feeling of, 'Oh my goodness, that's me.' There may have been other times where you've said, 'No, that's not me, but I can see that in other people.' If so, this is because Tom is multifaceted.

I hope that this journey through the Vaccine with Tom has given you food for thought. As I leave you now, there are three words that I urge you to keep in your mind whenever you're leading people and putting in place any of the Leadership Vaccine tools, hints, tips and insights. These are:

- Connection

- Clarity

- Commitment

As a leader, your ultimate aim is to build connection to your purpose, your role and your people. My connection to my purpose in the pharmaceutical industry was incredibly strong. I never had to ask myself, 'Why do I have to go in to work?'

The change in how Tom approached his role changed his business, but more importantly, it changed the careers, opportunities and lives of the people who work for him. We saw a disinterested Tom, who would walk into an office full of people he saw as resources where nobody even said hi to him, transform into a leader who was interested in and cared for his team. In fact, he became part of a team that he could rely on, learn from and build the business with.

That same connection to your own people will not only change you in terms of your leadership success, it will also allow you to enjoy your role and feel that you are a leader of people, rather than a leader of responsibility and fear. We've seen how vital it is to have clarity on your direction, scope and the boundaries of your role and responsibilities. Be clear with your teams on where you're heading and what is it that you're actually building together. Be clear on what is it that you do and what the roles and responsibilities of you and your teams are. Allow people to come in and jump straight into their work.

Once you and your teams have that connection and clarity, you'll find your collective commitment to your goals, each other and your customers will rise exponentially. Knowing that you can rely on those around you, and that everybody in your team knows who does what, you create the environment where people can put their hand up if they're not clear. When your people feel like they are heard by their leader, they are more committed to you, each other and the business.

Appendix

The Leadership VACCINE

The Five Pillars of Team Excellence

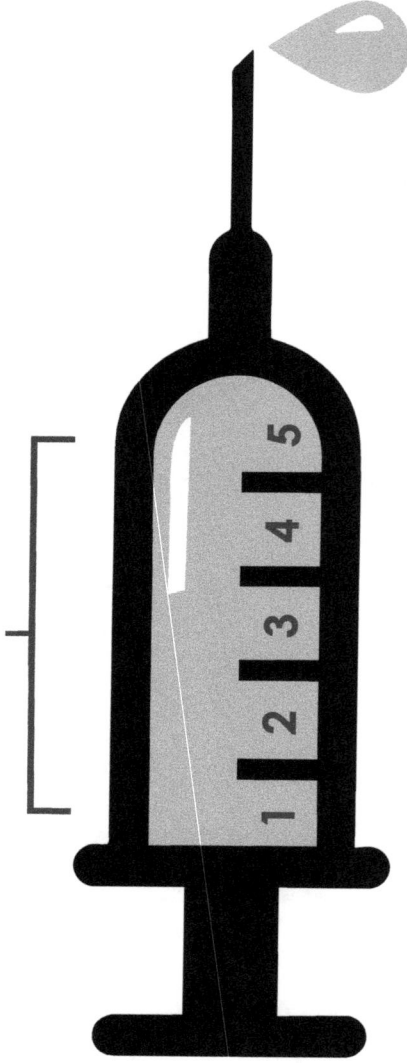

Value
your strengths, understand blind-spots and develop empathy for others

Advocate
for the right culture in your team

Clarify
the scope and boundaries of your team's responsibilities and activities

Create
the right organisation structure

Inspire
and activate your team with excellent staff development opportunities

eNable
your team to develop robust, efficient and future-proofed end-to-end processes

Execute
regular reviews to ensure ongoing team development and re-setting as needed

References

Andersen, E S, Grude, K V, Haug, T, *Goal Directed Project Management: Effective techniques and strategies* (Kogan Page, 2009, fourth edn)

Appelo, J, *Managing for Happiness: Games, tools, and practices to motivate any team* (John Wiley & Sons, 2016)

Harvey, J B, 'The Abilene Paradox: The management of agreement', *Organizational Dynamics* (1988), Summer Volume, pp 17–43

Hersey, P, *The Situational Leader* (Center for Leadership Studies Inc., 1984)

Herzberg, F, 'One More Time – How do you motivate your employees?' *Harvard Business Review* (2003), January, pp 2–13

International Standard ISO 9000, *Quality management systems – Fundamentals and vocabulary* (2015, fourth edn)

Jaques, E, *The Changing Culture of a Factory* (Routledge, 2001, reprinted edn)

Janis, I L, 'Groupthink', *Psychology Today* (1971), November, pp 84–90

Jung, C G, *Psychological Types* (Routledge, 2017)

Landsberg, M, *The Tao of Coaching: Boost your effectiveness at work by inspiring and developing those around you* (Harper Collins, 1996)

Lexico (2020) www.lexico.com

Ohno, T, 'Ask "Why" Five Times about Every Matter' (2006), www.toyota-myanmar.com/about-toyota /toyota-traditions/quality/ask-why-five-times-about -every-matter

Thomas, K W, *Intrinsic Motivation at Work: What really drives employee engagement* (Berrett-Koehler Publishers Inc., 2009, second edn)

Tuckman, B W, 'Developmental Sequence in Small Groups', *Psychological Bulletin* (1965), 63(6), pp 384–399

Acknowledgements

Writing this book has brought back to me the many challenges we face as leaders and has served as a reminder of the incredible support that I have received from friends and family for many years, not least of all this past year as I built my new business and wrote this book.

To my ever patient, supportive and insightful husband, Mark, thank you for your belief in me and my vision, not only now but for the past eighteen years. Thank you for being the calm, sensible one and for reading, re-reading and re-reading again these pages. Your opinion is something I hold in great esteem and so having your critical eye over the pages was invaluable, not only to the content but also to the confidence I have in my work. I am so pleased that on that day back in 2001 I was working as a waitress in a cocktail bar when I saw you!

To my boys, my beautiful Ethan and Theo, what can I say other than I think you are both brilliant human beings who bring so much good into this world. Thank you for being such kind, crazy and hilarious boys, I am so proud and lucky to be your mummy. Thank you Ethan for being my cheerleader, reminding me of what's important in life and for your awesome motivational quotes! Theo – thank you for your cuddles, laughs and funny faces.

To my mum – although you left us long before I became a leader and at a time when I was a million miles away from writing this book, I know you wouldn't have been surprised because you always believed that I would do big things, without you this book and its message wouldn't have been possible. Your audacity, authenticity and fun live on and continue to inspire how I lead, build my business and my life. I hope wherever you are, you are raising a glass with me!

To my dad, thank you firstly for lending your name to our lead character Tom. I named him after you as you were always someone who really challenged me as a leader. Whenever I had a challenge or a failure, you'd simply ask, 'But Beck, were you a good egg?' Dad, you were always my best critic, supporter and guide. I think you would have loved this book; I miss you so very much.

To the best mother-in-law a girl could wish for, Terri: thank you for being the best grandparent and parent Mark, I and the kids could wish for you. Your continued support and guidance make everything we do and achieve possible. Having you in my life has changed my life for the better in so many ways, I love you so very much.

To my simply awesome sister-in-law, Michelle, thanks for your ongoing support and great humour. You remind me that life is too short, and that balance is so important if we are to be truly happy.

To Daniel Priestley, thank you for making me believe that I had a book in me, for allowing me to acknowledge and own my mountain of value and inspiring me to make one hell of a Dent in this universe!

To Lucy, Joe, Helen, Alison and, of course, my brilliant book coach Mike at Rethink – thank you for your support, guidance and expertise. Mike, thank you for encouraging and inspiring me to use the story of Tom as a vehicle to deliver my message. I know we said that after this we would miss Tom – well, I will miss working with you too... until book two that is!

To Sapna at Innervisions ID, thank you for helping me to find the voice and tone of my brand, and for bringing yellow into my life! Your talent, expertise, passion and friendship has allowed me to deeply connect with and communicate what my business stands for, how I operate and who I serve. It has also allowed me draw a path of my own and truly allow myself to stand out.

Finally, I want to thank all the wonderful people I have had the great fortune to lead and learn from, in particular Amanda, Finn, Rita, Mary, Dami, Lori and Diane. Thank you for your partnership, friendship, and for the many laughs along the way. You are incredible at what you do, and it was an honour to play a small part in your journeys.

The Author

Rebecca Godfrey is the founder of Etheo Limited, a Team & Leadership Transformation consultancy, established in 2017 with the aim of 'Changing the way highly regulated industries operate'.

Rebecca is a scientist by background, having completed a PhD in Immunology at the University of Cambridge. Since leaving academic research, Rebecca's career has given her the opportunity to build and develop a successful drug safety consultancy business, work with and lead colleagues from more than ninety countries, live and work abroad and lead organisations and groups in roles ranging from Company Director of a small consultancy to Global Head and Global Director roles in two of the world's top ten pharma companies.

Having thoroughly enjoyed a fruitful and successful career so far, Rebecca took the leap to set up Etheo, bringing her wealth of business experience, outstanding leadership skills, strategy and process development expertise and passion for meeting new challenges, to support individuals and leaders to build cohesive, high performing teams with a focus on operational excellence.

Find Rebecca online at:

⊕ www.etheolimited.com

in https://www.linkedin.com/in/rebecca-godfrey -etheo/